Under the Same Roof

GUIDELINES (REVISED 1994)
to the
SHARING OF CHURCH BUILDINGS ACT, 1969

Published by the Council of Churches for Britain and Ireland
in association with
Churches Together in England and
CYTUN (Churches Together in Wales)

ISBN 0 85169 233 8
© 1994 Council of Churches for Britain and Ireland

Appendix III Sharing of Church Buildings 1969
© 1978 Crown copyright: reproduced by permission of HMSO

Published by CCBI
Inter-Church House
35-41 Lower Marsh
London SE1 7RL

Typeset and printed by Stanley L. Hunt (Printers) Ltd
Midland Road, Rushden, Northants

Ref JC 292

Contents

Contents

Foreword

The Sharing of Church Buildings Act became law in England and Wales in 1969. Circulars and Guidelines to help churches to take advantage of the Act were issued by the Churches' Main Committee, the Churches' Unity Commission and the British Council of Churches in 1970, 1974 and 1977. The latest revision was prepared by an ecumenical group under the BCC and issued in 1983.

These Guidelines are now out of print, and much has happened since 1983 that calls for a new edition.

Many more denominations have been gazetted, in order to enable their local churches to take advantage of the provisions of the Act. Many more local churches have entered into formal sharing agreements. The Council of Churches for Britain and Ireland has replaced the British Council of Churches, CYTUN has replaced the Council of Churches for Wales and Churches Together in England has been formed.

This publication distils all this experience and provides up to date guidance for churches at national, county/metropolitan area and local levels who want to know how to take advantage of the Act's provisions.

We are very grateful to the members of the Working Group (see Appendix V) for these Guidelines. The Act continues to provide a helpful framework for committed collaboration. We believe that *Under the Same Roof* offers clear advice for developing imaginative inter-church relationships within the Act, and we commend it to the Churches.

Martin Reardon
General Secretary
Churches Together
in England

Noel Davies
General Secretary
CYTUN:
Churches Together in Wales

Foreword

Introduction

This publication is intended for those in positions of leadership in the churches at local or wider level who are seriously considering negotiating a Sharing Agreement under the Sharing of Church Buildings Act, 1969. It is hoped that it will be of use also to

- legal advisers to the churches
- church officers with special responsibility for the proper use of buildings, e.g. Archdeacons, Circuit Superintendents
- ecumenical officers and members of ecumenical sponsoring bodies.

It is important to recognise that a Sharing Agreement under the Sharing of Church Buildings Act is only one of the ways in which buildings can be shared. Other approaches may, in any given circumstances, be more appropriate. More general advice on the shared use of buildings can be found in "The Sharing and Sale of Church Buildings – Report of a Working Party for Churches Together in England, 1993" which relates particularly to the special concerns of black majority and Oriental Orthodox Churches in London. The Interdenominational Consultative Committee on Ministry in Wales has also produced a leaflet encouraging churches to consider various forms of sharing, of which a Sharing Agreement under the Act is one (see Bibliography, Appendix IV).

Churches are at different points on the ecumenical pilgrimage. Where they are will affect their perception of what sharing a building should involve. This means that expectations are not always well-matched. If a Methodist and a United Reformed church decide to share a building there is likely to be an expectation that shared ministry and shared congregational life will be a natural part of the package. On the other hand a church within the Orthodox family sharing an Anglican church will expect to have its own times of worship, ministry from its own priest etc., though occasional opportunities for shared prayer or social events may be welcomed if language barriers are not perceived to be insuperable. Clearly the area from which the congregation is drawn will be much larger than the Anglican parish. Black majority churches will need to affirm their distinctiveness but may be happy to engage in joint worship from time to time and to join in or to initiate shared action with their partner church to meet some specific social need.

Sharing Agreements do not create "unified" churches. In some cases a Sharing Agreement may be seen simply as a necessary step to enable non-Anglican weddings to take place in an Anglican church. That may be all that is looked for. On the other hand proximity – rather than absence – can sometimes make the heart grow fonder. Opportunities for growing together in congregational life and witness will often present themselves. Churches who thought that their own life would continue as normal may discover that there is much more that can be shared besides a building.

1 The Origins and Use of the 1969 Act

In 1964 the British Council of Churches' Faith and Order Conference at Nottingham passed a resolution which called for its member churches "to designate areas of ecumenical experiment, at the request of local congregations or in new towns and housing areas. In such areas there should be experiment in ecumenical group ministries, in sharing buildings and equipment and in the development of mission" (*Unity Begins at Home*, SCM Press 1964, page 79). This was set in the wider context of the 1952 Lund Dictum which challenged the churches to "act together in all matters except those in which deep differences of conviction compel them to act separately" (*The Third World Conference on Faith and Order*, Lund 1952, ed. O. Tomkins, SCM Press 1953, page 16).

An initiative was taken to facilitate at the practical and legal level what was envisaged in the Nottingham resolution for areas of ecumenical experiment. In 1968 the Church of England, in close consultation with other churches, promoted a bill to authorise the sharing of church buildings by any two or more churches within England and Wales. This resulted in the Sharing of Church Buildings Act, 1969. In view of the Church of England's legal and constitutional position as the Established Church in England, the 1969 Act is worded to take account of its special status alongside, and sometimes in contrast to, the position of all other churches.

The Sharing of Church Buildings Act enables churches in England and Wales to enter into sharing agreements with regard to existing or new church buildings (including church halls, youth clubs and residences for ministers, clergy and lay workers). Similar provisions apply in Jersey by virtue of legislation by the States of Jersey in 1973 and in the Isle of Man by an Act of Tynwald in 1986. No such legislation exists for Scotland, Ireland, or Guernsey.

At the end of the nineteenth century and into the early twentieth century a number of congregationally ordered local churches promoted Acts of Parliament to enable the creation of united free churches –

1

Baptist/Congregational. However, most sharing (with the exception of that which was possible between locally autonomous congregations) in England and Wales had to operate either on the basis of an informal mutual understanding or by a more formalised arrangement in which one party was clearly the owner of the site and all buildings on it, and the other only a tenant or licensee. Sometimes such sharing was based on a generous interpretation of the law or on turning a blind eye to certain denominational regulations.

The passing of the 1969 Act, by providing a new legal basis for sharing, also introduced a new style of partnership within inter-church **relationships** in England and Wales. For some, the motivation for sharing buildings comes from a desire for closer ecumenical relations and work. For others, pragmatic considerations, such as temporary sharing during an emergency or the simple need for a place to meet, have led to closer ecumenical involvement between "host" and "guest" congregations.

In 1973 the title "Local Ecumenical Project" began to replace "Areas of Ecumenical Experiment". Given the growth of Local Ecumenical Projects in the 1970s and 1980s, and the movement to create local "Churches Together in . . ." in the 1990s, the 1969 Sharing of Church Buildings Act has continued to facilitate local ecumenism in one particular way "where there is at the level of the local church a formal, written agreement affecting the ministry, congregational life and/or buildings of more than one denomination; and a recognition of that agreement by the appropriate denominational authorities" (*Local Church Unity, Guidelines for Local Ecumenical Projects and Sponsoring Bodies*, BCC 1985, page 4).

Despite the changes and developments in the ecumenical scene locally and nationally over the last twenty or more years, the Sharing of Church Buildings Act of 1969 is the only legislation concerning this matter which has received the assent of all the major denominations in England and Wales and of Parliament; and it is probable that in its present form the Sharing of Church Buildings Act 1969 will continue to play this role in the foreseeable future, without substantial amendment or supplement, except through the continued extension of the list of Churches which fall within its provisions.

From 1st September 1990 the Council of Churches for Britain and Ireland came into existence with a new constitution as the legal successor to the British Council of Churches. Its Constitution (Article II 2 j) states that "the CCBI shall seek to further its objects by . . . continuing to perform such functions and to discharge such responsibilities as have been given to or imposed upon CCBI under its former name of the British Council of Churches and are deemed appropriate by CCBI's member churches". Among these functions are the provisions of the Sharing of Church Buildings Act 1969 Section 11(3), whereby

> "Any Church for the the time being represented on the General Council of the British Council of Churches or on the governing body of the Evangelical Alliance or the British Evangelical Council may give notice in writing to the General Secretary of the British Council of Churches or as the case may be of the governing body concerned, that it desires that this Act should apply to that Church, and the notice shall specify the appropriate authority or authorities of that Church for the purposes of this Act, and the General Secretary concerned shall publish in the *London Gazette* a notice signed by him –
>
> (a) stating that the Church concerned is represented on the said General Council or governing body and has expressed its desire that this Act should apply to that Church;
>
> (b) stating that this Act will apply to that Church as from the date of the publication of the notice; and
>
> (c) specifying the appropriate authority or authorities of that Church for the purpose of this Act;
>
> and thereupon this Act shall apply to that Church as from that date."

A list of Churches to which the Act applies is set out in chapter 12.

According to the CCBI Constitution Article IV "The Assembly and Church Representatives Meeting . . . together constitute the Governing Body of CCBI. The Governing Body constitutes the General Council for the purposes of the Sharing of Church Buildings Act 1969, the CCBI being the legal successor to the BCC."

The CCBI Co-ordinating Secretary for Church Life handles applications under this Section and arranges for eligible churches to be gazetted so that the Act may apply to them. This involves provision of the details required and the payment of the fee required by the *London Gazette* for miscellaneous Public Notices (currently about £45.00) which may be shared between two or three churches making a simultaneous application.

Applications by churches represented on the governing body of the Evangelical Alliance or of the British Evangelical Council are currently handled respectively by the General Director, Evangelical Alliance, Whitfield House, 186 Kennington Park Road, London SE1 4BT, and the General Secretary, British Evangelical Council, 113 Victoria Street, St. Albans, Hertfordshire AL1 3TJ.

In England, once a church has been gazetted and come within the terms of the Sharing of Church Buildings Act, 1969, it may also become eligible to be designated under the Church of England's legislation, the Church of England (Ecumenical Relations) Measure, 1988, and Canons B43 and B44, which provide legal authority for certain types of local ecumenical co-operation, in particular as regards the participation of Anglican and non-Anglican clergy and lay people in each other's worship.

No sharing agreement may be made with respect to a cathedral church or peculiar (including a collegiate church) of the Church of England. However, the Act does authorise a dean or provost and chapter of a Church of England cathedral to authorise the use of a chapel or other part of the cathedral for worship in accordance with the forms of service of two or more of the churches to which the Act applies.

Similarly, although a sharing agreement may not be made with respect to a church building of the Church of England situated in an extra-diocesan or extra-parochial place, authority is given in the Act for the building to be used by two or more of the churches to which the Act applies (see Section 10 of the Act).

No sharing agreement may be made in respect of a school or land used or appropriated for use for burials (see Section 12 of the Act).

2 The Advantages of a Sharing Agreement

There are a number of ways in which a building owned by one church can be used by another. These include a lease or licence; a "gentleman's agreement"; emergency arrangements in the wake of fire damage etc; and arrangements under the Ecumenical Canons B43 & B44 of the Church of England. However the advantages of a formal sharing agreement are considerable.

Subject to the necessary legal requirements, a Sharing Agreement can be made which will enable:

(a) flexibility in worship, work and witness which would otherwise be impossible because of the trusts on which a building is held;

(b) certain funds to be transferred across denominational boundaries for certain purposes; for example proceeds of sale from the building of one denomination or other capital money can be used in the building of another;

(c) security of tenure (within the terms of the Sharing Agreement) which will specify a period of notice – usually six months minimum – to be given to members of one denomination who leave their own building to worship in the shared building;

(d) marriage services to be conducted according to the rites and ceremonies of the denominations who are parties to the Sharing Agreement;

(e) residences for ministers or lay workers, church halls or centres and youth clubs or youth hostels to be shared as well as buildings for worship.

Except where specific exclusions are made by the Act, Sharing Agreements are binding upon successors and enable the rites, ceremonies and practices of one denomination to be used in a building where the legal requirements, other than any covenants affecting the legal holding of the body owning that building, may seem specifically to exclude that rite or practice. For example, in a Methodist building which is the subject of a Sharing Agreement with the Church of England, the normal practice in the Church of England of using fermented wine at the service of Holy Communion may be followed. Or again, in a Baptist Church which is the subject of a Sharing Agreement, infant baptisms may be held according to the tradition(s) of the other church(es) sharing the building.

For worshippers, the sharing of a building often leads to fellowship across the denominational divide and a growing desire for closer co-operation in worship, work and witness.

3   Possible Problems

Sharing a building is often a good use of resources – good stewardship. But beware. Is one church primarily looking for a way to avoid closure? Is another church wanting a short-term base while amassing funds to secure its own building? The parties must be frank with each other, and make sure that the terms of the Agreement are appropriate to the legitimate aspirations of both (all).

Is there an agreed intention to extend/alter/rebuild the premises? It has been known for a "guest" church to enter into a Sharing Agreement on this understanding, only to discover that the "host" church, having secured more funding to maintain the building, no longer wishes to proceed with a more radical solution. The "guest" church may feel cheated. The rights of the "guest" church will not of course extend to such matters as lettings to third parties, undertaking structural alterations and sale of part or all of the property.

As far as possible it is important to ascertain whether sharing is expected to be temporary, long-term or permanent, since the 1969 Act is not intended for short-term sharing. However, a sudden emergency may have led one congregation to offer hospitality to or seek it from another on a short-term basis – during rebuilding after fire damage, for example. In such circumstances two congregations may simply co-exist in the one building, putting up with a measure of mutual inconvenience, or they may seek to integrate aspects of their life and worship. But it has been known for both churches then to move together under a Sharing Agreement into the newly refurbished building of the guest church.

Problems can arise because of the need to leave reasonable time for one congregation to follow another at their agreed times of worship.

Experience has shown that some local churches are too "fragile" to enter into a Sharing Agreement. It is particularly important that the host church should have an assured future. It is not necessary for the congregations to be equivalent in numbers/financial resources but both parties will need to be reasonably confident that this can be a partnership and not a take-over.

Even so, over time one partner may become so weak that its viability is in question. Where one of the partner churches is congregationally governed and all the key decisions are taken by a Church Meeting (e.g. Congregational Federation churches, Baptist churches) it has been noted that on some rare occasions after a few years it becomes difficult to identify a Church Meeting capable of giving and receiving notices as may be required by the Sharing Agreement. It is, therefore, suggested that in the clauses which refer to the Church Meeting giving or receiving notices an additional sentence is added on the following lines:

"Where the number of identifiable church members falls below three notice under this clause may be given by (the Baptist Association in which the church is situated/the Congregational Federation Area in which the church is situated)."

Once problems are recognised, those concerned can together set about seeking solutions to them, and this may result in greater mutual understanding and growth together, even though negotiations may be protracted.

While it is particularly important to remember that the Act can provide a framework within which churches can develop ways of working and worshipping together more closely, a Sharing Agreement is only one of the possible steps towards deeper Christian Unity.

4   Ten Steps Towards a Sharing Agreement

Certain churches have availed themselves of the Act again and again since it came into operation and have established precedents and procedures which enable local churches to draw on this denominational wisdom. Provided that the local churches do not insist on substantial variations in the clauses, it is possible to proceed with the minimum of cost and of delay. The Methodist Church and the United Reformed Church have particular expertise in this area and Methodist/URC sharing presents little problem.

The Ten Steps set out below will be of particular value to churches which do not have clearly worked out procedures and which have not built up expertise at national or diocesan (or equivalent) level.

Since local situations differ, the actual process of producing a Sharing Agreement varies somewhat. These ten steps suggest a possible order of operation. Each of these steps needs to be included at some point in the process if later difficulties are to be avoided.

1.   Consult Widely at an Early Stage –

(a)   The appropriate denominational leaders (whether at local or inter-mediate level);

(b)   the ordinary members of the congregations likely to be affected, pointing out frankly the major implications, advantages and disad-vantages mentioned above; make available copies of the Churches Together in England leaflet *What is a Shared Building?* (available from CTE offices at £5.00 per 100 + p & p);

(c)   the denominational ecumenical officers for your area, who will have useful expertise;

(d)   those within the structures of the Church who will have to give various formal Consents later (see chapter 13, PARTIES AND CONSENTS);

(e)   in the case of churches in England, the secretary of the Intermedi-ate/County/Metropolitan Sponsoring Body;

(f)   other churches in your area where a Sharing Agreement is already in operation.

2.   **Read:** These Guidelines *including the Act itself* and

> **A Harmony of Church Administration –**
> Basil W. Hazledine, BCC 1990, which sets out (pages 24-27) procedures and responsibilities for Sharing Agreements within The Baptist Union of Great Britain, Church of England, Methodist, Roman Catholic and United Reformed Churches (available from CCBI Bookroom, £5.95 + p & p).

3.   **Agree with your own appropriate Church Authorities** the general pattern of the Sharing Agreement that fits your needs best. This pattern should arise out of the consultation in step 2 above. The more general the terms of the Agreement the greater will be your freedom to use the opportunities it gives for the congregations to develop their life together later. The Agreement should **not** cover detailed constitutions, declarations of intent and patterns or times of worship. If such are desired they must be dealt with quite separately from the Agreement itself. It is important to recognise the distinction between the documents.

    The Encyclopaedia of Forms and Precedents, to which every solicitor has access, contains precedents for Sharing Agreements, which do not therefore have to be drawn up from scratch each time. This should be borne in mind not least by smaller churches with limited resources (see Appendix II for examples of Sharing Agreements).

4.   **Talk with appropriate Solicitors** about the procedures involved, unless the appropriate denominational authorities authorise otherwise. Church of England parishes should normally consult their diocesan registrar. The Property Division of the Methodist Church is able to act for Methodist managing trustees in the preparation of certain Sharing Agreements, and most URC Provinces can provide a similar service for United Reformed Churches. Some solicitors are recommended by denominational authorities. This has the advantage that they are building up a body of expertise in using the Act. **The temptation to save costs by "doing it yourself" without solicitors should be resisted.** It is also important that each party to the Agreement has its own solicitor – one solicitor should not act for all. Having a solicitor for each is the

best way of fully safeguarding the interests of everybody involved. Be clear which **one** person in each denomination will be the official contact with that denomination's solicitor.

5. **Be Realistic about Costs and Timetable.** The costs of the Sharing Agreement will normally have to be borne by the local Churches involved, and should be budgeted for. It is important to remember that even a simple agreement (between just two churches) will take at least five to six hours of a lawyer's time when necessary correspondence is included, and **every extra variation adds to the costs for each party concerned.** It is essential to discuss with the solicitors at an early stage the work they will do and the charges that will be incurred. While many Sharing Agreements are effected within six to nine months, between one and two years may be needed, especially if there are several churches involved. Not infrequently a Church of England incumbent moves during the process and it may not be possible for an Agreement to be signed until the vacancy is filled.

6. **The Church "Owning" the Building involved instructs its Solicitors** to prepare a draft which will translate your wishes into an appropriate form of words – unless what you want is not legally possible! Where joint ownership of a building is involved, a more complex situation arises (see chapter 11, JOINT OWNERSHIP).

7. **The Solicitors of the "Owning" Church agree the Form of the Draft** with the solicitors of the other church or churches involved. There is likely to be a need for several drafts before all requirements are adequately met. Where several churches are involved, especially if they are unsure of their expectations and requirements or change their minds mid-stream, this may be a lengthy and expensive process. Using experienced solicitors is highly recommended.

8. **The necessary Consents must be obtained** to the Agreement before it can be signed.

9. The Parties concerned **execute the Agreement,** it is formally **registered** in the office of each of the appropriate authorities (see Section 1(8) of the Act) and **comes into operation.** In a few cases formal registration has been overlooked, and therefore the document has no legal force. It is unwise for any church to sign building contracts before the Agreement has been signed and registered unless it can cover the whole capital cost of the work.

10. The Building should be certified under the Places of Worship Registration Act 1855, if appropriate. If it is to be used for marriages according to the rites of the guest church(es), registration and authorisation will be needed, so the local Superintendent Registrar must be approached and shown the completed Sharing Agreement. If the "guest" church is Anglican, the bishop will normally license the building for Anglican marriages. If a completely new building is involved early consultation with the Registrar is recommended to avert later problems.

If the predominant use of the building is as a community centre rather than for worship, early consultation is also advisable.

The rest of this publication provides more detailed information on what is involved in these steps.

5   Trust and Sensitivity

The ten steps towards a Sharing Agreement set out above underline the importance of thorough preparation and careful drafting of documents which will be legally binding on those parties on whose behalf they are signed. Goodwill on its own on the part of those eager to secure an immediate working agreement will not be sufficient. Stronger safeguards are needed to ensure that their best intentions will be maintained in the future by those who may not always appreciate the background to the agreement.

The counter-balance to this painstaking drafting is the high degree of trust and sensitivity that is equally essential for the operation of a satisfactory agreement. This means taking time to build relationships between ministers and congregations **before** any formal agreement is considered. It also means becoming reasonably familiar with a wide variety of practices and expectations from the different congregations and denominations involved. It is particularly important to remember that while the Act provides a **framework** within which churches can develop ways of working and worshipping together more closely, a Sharing Agreement by itself does not constitute a "unified church".

This will be appreciated when consideration is given to the areas of common interest dealt with in chapters 6 to 11, in all of which mutual understanding and sympathy are of paramount importance.

6   The Joint Council

Model Sharing Agreements almost invariably provide for the constitution of a Joint Council representing the sharing churches and, although such a Council is not strictly required by the Act, it is highly desirable that one should be set up (see Appendix II(a) Clause 2 for example of functions and Second Schedule for example of composition).

The Joint Council will have a particularly important role in situations where integration of congregational life is not envisaged. Where there is integration and an Ecumenical Council is constituted (with the full endorsement of the denominational authorities and sponsoring body) the Joint Council's role may diminish but the Joint Council must still be iden‑ tifiable so that it can be called if necessary.

The usual functions of the Joint Council are these:

(a)   To settle any questions which may arise regarding the respective times at which the sharing churches are to have the use of the church building.

(b)   To advise those responsible for the management, maintenance and repair of the church buildings on behalf of the congregations of the sharing churches regarding financial questions and particularly regarding any exceptional expenditure (see Appendix II(a) for matters normally specified as common costs of management; note that these include insurance).

(c)   To organise or to consider and if thought fit to approve proposals for the raising of such common funds as are to be raised jointly by the congregations acting together.

(d)   Generally to facilitate joint action and the settlement of questions of detail which may arise in the carrying out of this Agreement.

The actual membership of the Council varies according to which churches are sharing the building. This point is one that needs careful discussion with legal advisers and Church authorities if misunderstandings are to be avoided. The convention of equal representation of the sharing churches is symbolic of their partnership.

It is also worth considering the chairing of the Council. Is it to revolve among the denominations involved – or can the Council be jointly chaired? Is it to be by named office holders – such as the incumbent or minister, or is it to be by some form of election? The decisions made about this can be important in developing real trust and sharing.

The Joint Council will need to meet at least once a year, if only formally, even if many matters relating to the building and finance are delegated to the Ecumenical Church Council. An annual meeting of the Joint Council need not be burdensome – if there is not much business it can meet before or after a meeting of the Ecumenical Church Council (where such exists). There will also be purposes for which denominational Church Councils are still necessary.

In England the advice of the Ecumenical Sponsoring Body (whose functions are usually now included in those of Intermediate/County Bodies) should always be sought when drawing up a constitution providing for an Ecumenical Church Council. In both England and Wales consultation will be necessary with the appropriate denominational authorities of each of the participating churches when seeking to integrate congregational life and/or ministry.

7 Denominational Worship and Joint Services

The aim of the 1969 Act is that in a Shared Building each denomination may do whatever would be permitted in its own building.

A Sharing Agreement should therefore make provision in the case of a shared building used as a place of worship for determining the extent to which it is to be available for worship in accordance with the forms of service of the sharing churches. It may also provide for the holding of joint services.

The phrase that appears in Section 4(1) of the Act, "such joint services on such occasions as may be approved by those Churches", may be interpreted in a variety of ways. In practice, however, whatever the wishes of the local congregations beginning to explore a closer relationship with each other, the pattern of "joint services" will need to respect the limits set by the denominational authorities involved, often operating through an Ecumenical Sponsoring Body.

The Trust Deed of a building may also restrict what may be done at a joint service, although use of the terms "occasional" or "normally" may offer some licence.

Most denominations rule that the nature of any service is determined by the denominational identity of the person conducting it. However, some ministers are now appointed to serve joint congregations or to have pastoral oversight of the congregation belonging to a denomination different from their own, and this means that fine distinctions as to whose worship it is cannot be made so easily. This is particularly true of the Free Churches in England and Wales. Moreover, the Church of England Canons B43 and B44 and the Church in Wales Ecumenical Canons 1990 offer further encouragement for local churches to plan an agreed pattern of joint services, and the Covenanted Churches in Wales have established and authorised a rite of Holy Communion and a common Baptismal Rite. In England a number of sponsoring bodies have approved the use of agreed services for joint Confirmation. A joint Confirmation Rite for use in Local

Ecumenical Projects was prepared by the Joint Liturgical Group in 1992.

The pattern of allowing greater flexibility in regulations governing worship is therefore developing in many ways. It is nevertheless important to take great care to ensure that the participating congregations **"own"** any joint service proposed. Worship should arise out of and further, deepen and develop the relationship of the congregations involved.

8 Congregational and Denominational Identity

Whatever is permitted in one denomination's own building may be done in the building belonging to another unless specifically excluded in the Sharing Agreement (see Sections 2(1) and 4(1) of the Act). This may be done without infringing any wider restrictions that may exist elsewhere in the owning denomination – in other words, it does not create a precedent to be followed in other places. Put at its simplest the provisions of the Act allow a "guest" church effectively to use the "host" church's building for the same specific activities including worship as it would use its own building. It may therefore follow its own rules which may be different from the rules of the host denomination.

Sensitivity however is needed where one of the congregations involved in a Sharing Agreement is much stronger in leadership or numbers than the other(s), since this may easily produce a perception of a "take-over bid", even if the smaller congregation is the owner of the building. Indeed, pride may work in two undermining ways to induce suspicion and stifle good relationships. A larger congregation may feel self-satisfied and consider the smaller potential partner to be an unwarranted liability; and a smaller congregation may feel its independence and identity to be threatened by a larger partner.

Decisions about the transfer of particular items of furniture, memorials, etc, from a church being closed to the one that is to be shared can be blighted by feelings of mistrust or careless disregard of special associations and sensitivities. The use of alcohol at church functions/wedding receptions etc may become a contentious issue unless a satisfactory policy is agreed from the outset. Differing policies at a denominational level may also prove awkward, such as varying attitudes regarding the re-marriage in church of divorced people whose previous partners are still living. It may even become impossible for any local agreement to proceed in advance of an agreed change at national level, and if this is so great care must be taken that relationships at the local level are not soured.

Notwithstanding the references above regarding marriages, one of the intentions of the 1969 Act is to permit marriages according to the practice of one denomination in the Shared Building belonging to another denomination **provided that it is registered for that purpose under the terms of Section 6 of the Act.**

Neither the 1969 Act nor the precedents prepared for Sharing Agreements define the degree of continuing denominational identity necessary beyond the creation of a Joint Council for which all the Model Sharing Agreements provide. This is usually set up under Schedule 2 of a Sharing Agreement, where the members are clearly appointed by the various churches involved, and these churches therefore have a continuing presence.

In some cases, however, there is such integration of congregational life and worship that a significant number of people come to understand themselves as belonging to a worshipping ecumenical congregation rather than to any of the denominations from which it is formed. However, it is important to make it clear that the sharing churches each remain a constituent part of their respective denominations. This fact may well be highlighted by the presence of representatives of the wider church on the Joint Council. Care must therefore be taken that any local Ecumenical Church Council does not take to itself powers that properly belong to the Joint Council unless the terms of the Sharing Agreement have been amended to authorise this.

9 Termination of Sharing Agreements and Security of Capital

A sharing agreement must contain provisions for terminating the sharing of church buildings. Such provisions may –

> (i) if the agreement relates to two or more buildings, provide for terminating the sharing of any building before the others;
> (ii) if there are more than two sharing churches, provide for the withdrawal of any church from the sharing of any church building, not being a church which is the sole owner or previous owner of the building;
> (iii) specify the financial adjustments as between the churches on such termination or withdrawal (see Section 9(1) of the Act).

On termination a building owned by one only of the sharing churches shall be held on the trusts or for the purposes on or for which it was held before the Sharing Agreement or would be held but for the Sharing Agreement (see Section 9(2) of the Act).

Where a building is jointly owned by all or some of the sharing churches (previously having been owned by one of those churches) it shall vest, on termination, without any conveyance in the incumbent of the parish in which the building is then situated (if it was previously a consecrated church of the Church of England) or in such of the trustees in whom the building is vested as represent the church who previously owned the buildings (see Section 9(3) of the Act).

Where a jointly owned building has not previously been owned by one only of the sharing churches, the Sharing Agreement may provide, on termination, for the disposal of the building, including disposal to one of the sharing churches, and for the application of the proceeds to charitable purposes of the sharing churches (see Section 9(4) of the Act).

What is usually Clause 6 in a Sharing Agreement provides for agreement to be reached as to the terms upon which capital monies may be accepted and whose consents are required. It has to be recognised that the Act leaves unresolved the matter of providing security for the money of one church put into the existing building of another denomination, whether church, hall or house, if for whatever reason the Sharing Agreement is terminated. This is because Section 9(2) of the Act states that if any Agreement comes to an end, the building **reverts** to being "held on the trusts . . . for which it was held before the Sharing Agreement" was entered into. In a majority of cases the host church will not wish to or be in a position to sell the property and it is therefore difficult for a guest partner to get capital back.

To anticipate this situation provision may be made in a Sharing Agreement (or in a separate subsequent document) for a legal charge on the church building in an agreed form to be entered into if and when the Sharing Agreement is terminated. Within these restrictions protection is afforded for the capital money that has been contributed by the guest church or churches, even if the Sharing Agreement is terminated.

It has been suggested that the best way of covering the trustee responsibility involved is for the Agreement to include a clause which places a first call on the proceeds of the sale of the property to be paid not on the termination of the Agreement but on the eventual sale of the property or site. The future of both (all) parties to such Agreement could be seriously jeopardised by the withdrawal of one of them if in order to repay capital monies the building had to be sold immediately. Where it is the owning denomination that wishes to terminate the Agreement and sell the building, courtesy requires that it be offered in the first instance to the "guest" church(es), subject, however, to the provisions of the Charities Act, 1993, (Sections 36 and 37) regarding dispositions of charity land.

A legal charge cannot, however, be made to apply to a consecrated Church of England building.

It should be noted that this sort of legal charge is very costly, involving extra work and the preparation of another document. In 1990 the Methodist Church and most United Reformed Church Provinces resolved that such a charge would not normally be made in a Simple Sharing Agreement between them relating to an existing place of worship, though a legal charge is often used when manses are subject to a Sharing Agreement.

We cannot emphasise too strongly that termination of a Sharing Agreement is almost always a painful experience.

10 Faculty Jurisdiction

All the parties involved in an Agreement need to be aware that the Act makes a special provision relating to the sharing of consecrated churches of the Church of England (see Section 5 of the Act). These remain subject to the Church of England Faculty Jurisdiction and to the system of quinquennial surveys. Faculty Jurisdiction applies to the fabric of the churches and to the movable contents belonging to the Church of England but not to the movable contents of another denomination brought into it. The Church in Wales has its own similar Faculty Jurisdiction. This means that all the other denominations involved in sharing such buildings must recognise the requirements of the Faculty Jurisdiction and the duties imposed on a Parochial Church Council by the system of quinquennial surveys.

Account needs to be taken of the Standing Orders, other regulations and requirements as to the Quinquennial or other Inspections, to which church buildings owned by all denominations are subject.

The Sharing Agreement will often relate to the whole property, including car park, gardens etc. In such cases responsibility for maintenance of these areas needs to be clearly stated. It must be remembered that a Sharing Agreement cannot be made in respect of a graveyard (see chapter 1, page 4).

11   Joint Ownership

For the great majority of cases, particularly those involving existing buildings and congregations, a "simple" Agreement, in which one church retains ownership of each building is strongly recommended. It can be produced far more quickly and at a much lower cost than one involving joint ownership and is sufficiently flexible to allow the fullest working and witnessing together of the denominations involved.

With respect to an existing consecrated church of the Church of England a Sharing Agreement may only be made if –

(i)   the church will remain in the sole ownership of the Church of England; or

(ii)   authority to make the agreement on behalf of the Church of England is given by a pastoral scheme under the Pastoral Measure, 1968, and the church will under the agreement be in the joint ownership of the Church of England and another church or churches (see Section 5 of the Act).

Where it is proposed to share an existing residence house of a benefice of the Church of England, authority to make the agreement on behalf of that church must be given under a pastoral scheme under the Pastoral Measure, 1983. These requirements do not apply to the Church in Wales.

However, there are situations, particularly those involving new developments, where joint ownership is appropriate. Joint ownership may also be the only way of dealing with the problem of providing security for the money from one denomination invested in the building of another since it allows for the selling of the property and an agreed division of the proceeds (see chapter 9, TERMINATION OF SHARING AGREEMENTS AND SECURITY OF CAPITAL).

Since the Act made possible joint ownership of buildings, various methods of achieving this have been evolved. Variation occurs principally on the issue of which body is chosen to act as Custodian Trustee for the property and how far the role of Managing Trustees is performed by the

Joint Council created by the Sharing Agreement. The legal representatives of the churches do not consider it right to commend a single method for joint ownership, partly because of the differing approaches and emphases of the denominations they represent and partly because local circumstances may make one method more suitable than another.

The methods of joint ownership may be broadly characterised as follows:

METHOD "A". Although jointly owned an appropriate corporate body in one denomination acts as Custodian Trustee. The fact that one denomination is thus seen as ultimate "owner" prevents some local projects from employing this method even though the Custodian Trustee is merely the custodian and is subject, like the local Managing Trustees, to the trusts on which the property is held. In so far as action is needed, the custodian acts on the direction of the Managing Trustees, usually functioning through the Joint Council created by the Sharing Agreement.

METHOD "B". The property is vested in local trustees nominated by the two or more churches involved in the scheme. This has the advantages of fairness in the eyes of all parties but has all the drawbacks of using individuals rather than some corporate body. There may be insufficient time to set up the body of trustees before contracts have to be exchanged on a purchase, particularly where a house is concerned. The constituting document should provide for the replacement of trustees by appropriate appointment.

METHOD "C". A Company Limited by Guarantee is formed under the Companies Acts of 1948 to 1989 with Directors appointed by the participating denominations. The Company acquires property, erects a building and gradually passes over responsibility to local Managing Trustees (usually the Joint Council) while retaining its function as Custodian Trustee. The advantages of the Company Limited by Guarantee are that it can be used in an area where there is new housing development but as yet no existing congregations and is flexible enough for responsibility to be devolved gradually to local people. There is a "One Shared Church Company" acting as Custodian Trustee for all "new" shared churches in the geographical diocese of Hertfordshire and Bedfordshire – at present it covers four such churches. It also has the advantage of limited liability. Its drawbacks are that the exercise is relatively costly and time-consuming and some complications can arise when Companies proliferate within the same Diocese or District.

FOOTNOTE: Not recommended any more –

A "neutral" office is chosen to act as Custodian Trustee, namely the Official Custodian for Charities. Again although the Official Custodian's functions and powers are extremely limited, some local congregations dislike the idea of involving "the State" in matters pertaining to the churches.

12 Churches to which The Act Applies, Authorities, Parties & Consents

There follows the **DATE** from which the Act has applied; the **NAME** of the church(es) concerned; the **APPROPRIATE AUTHORITIES** required by the Act to be designated as those responsible (a) for determining who the parties to a particular sharing agreement shall be, i.e. who actually signs it; and whose consents shall be required for it, i.e. whose approval must formally be obtained according to the church's polity before the sharing agreement can be signed; and (b) for keeping a register of sharing agreements; the **PARTIES** so determined; and the **CONSENTS** required before a sharing agreement can be entered into.

	Date	Name of Church(es)	Appropriate Authorities	Parties	Consents
1.	1969	Any Church of the Baptist Denomination*	(a) The Baptist Trust Corporation† with the concurrence of the Church Meeting (b) The Baptist Trust Corporation	The Baptist Union Corporation Ltd or other trustees	The Baptist Church Meeting
2.	1969	Any Church of the Congregational Denomination*	(a) The Trust Corporation† with the concurrence of the Church Meeting (b) The Trust Corporation	The Trust Corporation	The Church Meeting
3.	1969	Church of England	(a) Parliament (b) Provincial and Diocesan Registry	The Diocesan Board of Finance and the Incumbent and Parochial Church Council‡	‡The Bishop and the Pastoral Committee

	Date	Name of Church(es)	Appropriate Authorities	Parties	Consents
4.	1969	Methodist Church	(a) The Annual Conference of the Methodist Church (b) The Methodist Church Property Division	The Connexional Ecumenical Officer, the Church Council, and, when the building belongs to the Methodist Church, the Trustees for Methodist Church Purposes	The Methodist Church Property Division and Connexional Ecumenical Committee together with approvals at local, Circuit and District levels
5.	1969	Roman Catholic Church in England and Wales	The Bishop of the Diocese	The Trustees	The Bishop of the Diocese
6.	1969	Church in Wales	The Governing Body of the Church in Wales	The Representative Body of the Church in Wales	The Bishop & Incumbent & Church Wardens & (in a conventional district) Priest in Charge
7.	1972	United Reformed Church	The Synod of the Province of the URC in which the church building(s) is/are/will be situated	Those determined by the Provincial Synod & the Trustees in whom an existing building is vested	The Provincial Synod or those determined by it
8.	1974	Congregational Federation	The Trust Corporation, known as the Congregational Federation Ltd	The Congregational Federation Ltd	The Church Meeting
9.	1974	Moravian Church	The Synod of the Moravian Church in the British Province	Moravian Union (Incorporated)	The Provincial Elders' Conference
10.	1975	Any Churches of Elim Foursquare Gospel Alliance	Elim Foursquare Gospel Alliance & Elim Trust Corporation	Elim Trust Corporation or appropriate local Trustees	Elim Foursquare Gospel Alliance Executive Council
11.	1977	Presbyterian Church of Wales	The General Assembly of the Presbyterian Church of Wales	The Properties Board of the Presbyterian Church of Wales	Associations in the North, East or South of the Presbyterian Church of Wales

	Date	Name of Church(es)	Appropriate Authorities	Parties	Consents
12.	1979	Any Congregation of the Fellowship of Churches of Christ in Great Britain & Ireland	(a) The Annual Conference of the Fellowship of Churches of Christ with the concurrence of the Church meeting (b) The Annual Conference of the Fellowship of Churches of Christ	Church Meeting	Annual Conference or Executive of the Christian Service Council
13.	1984	Shiloh United Church of Christ Apostolic (Worldwide)	National Executive Board	Local Pastor National/International Coordinator	Local Church Meeting
14.	1984	International Ministerial Council of Great Britain	IMCGB Executive Committee	Department of Theology & Law	The Board of Bishops
15.	1985	Archdiocese of Thyateira and Great Britain (Greek Orthodox Church)	The Archbishop of Thyateira and Great Britain	The Archbishop of Thyateira and Great Britain	The parish priest & the President of the Community on behalf of the Administrative Committee
16.	1989	The Salvation Army	The Salvation Army Trustee Company	Territorial Headquarters	Territorial Headquarters
17.	1989	Council of Oriental Orthodox Christian Churches	The Chairman of the Council	The Chairman of the Council	
18.	1989	Chinese Church in London	The Church Council	The Church Council	The Church Meeting
19.	1990	Lutheran Council of Great Britain	Chairman of the Council	Chairman of the Council	
20.	1991	The Free Church of England	The Church Council represented by the General Secretary	The Diocesan Council as appropriate	The Bishop of the appropriate Diocese

	Date	Name	Appropriate Authorities	Parties	Consents
21.	1991	New Testament Assembly	The Executive Board of NTA	The National Overseer, the General Secretary & the Local Minister	NTA Executive Committee, Trustees, The Church Council
22.	1991	Council of African & Afro-Caribbean Churches	The Chairman of the Council		
23.	1991	The Oakes Christian Fellowship, Sheffield	The Leadership Team	The Leadership Team	The Leadership Team
24.	1991	Southam Road Evangelical Fellowship, Banbury	The Church Trustees represented by the General Secretary	The Church Trustees	The Church Meeting
25.	1991	New Testament Church of God	The National Overseer	The National Executive Council & National Secretary	The Church Meeting
26.	1991	Old Baptist Union	The General Secretary	The Council of Management	The Church Meeting
27.	1992	Joint Council of Anglo-Caribbean Churches	The General Secretary of the Joint Council		
28.	1992	Cherubim and Seraphim Council of Churches	The General Secretary of the Council		
29.	1994	Independent Methodist Churches	(a) The Connexional Committee represented by the General Secretary (b) The Independent Methodist Association Inc	The General Secretary	The Independent Methodist Church Meeting

31

Notes

* These titles include churches of a Baptist/Congregational polity regardless of whether or not they are in membership with any Baptist/Congregational/Independent Union or Federation, and include, for instance, any Welsh Congregational Church.

† For the purpose of this Schedule, "the Baptist Trust Corporation" and "the Congregational Trust Corporation" have the following meanings:

(a) if the church building or buildings to which the sharing agreement concerned relates is or are or will be vested in a Baptist or Congregational Trust Corporation within the meaning of the Baptist and Congregational Trusts Act, 1951, it means that Corporation;

(b) otherwise it means the Baptist or Congregational Trust Corporation (within the meaning of the said Act) in whose area of operations the church building or buildings is or are or will be situated, or if there is more than one such Corporation, the one determined by the Church Meeting;

(c) in the case of the Undeb yr Annibynwyr Cymraeg (Union of Welsh Independents) the Appropriate Authorities are the Trustees with the concurrence of the Church Meeting and the Parties are the Union of Welsh Independents Incorporated (if it serves as an Incorporated Trustee of the local church) and/or local trustees.

‡ Different provisions apply in some special cases, e.g. where there is no incumbent or bishop or where the building is held on certain education trusts.

NB: Requests for information about churches gazetted after the publication of these Guidelines should be addressed to the Co-ordinating Secretary for Church Life, CCBI, Inter-Church House, 35-41 Lower Marsh, London SE1 7RL.

Appendix 1
Glossary

Terms which are used frequently by and are familiar to those in one church tradition or within a particular discipline (e.g. solicitors) may mean little or nothing to those from a different background. This is particularly the case in a booklet dealing with the legal position of a variety of churches.

An attempt is made here, therefore, to give a simple definition or explanation of some of the terms used in the foregoing pages which may not readily be understood by everyone. For obvious reasons it is impracticable to be exhaustive and for the sake of brevity some generalisations are necessary, and this glossary is for guidance only. Terms in heavy type are cross-referenced.

(1969) ACT

This is the **Sharing of Church Buildings Act, 1969,** which sets out the provisions for formal, legal **sharing** of church **buildings** (see chapter 1). An Act of Parliament was needed to enable the established Church of England to share premises with other **churches,** but it makes provision for churches of all **denominations** which have been **gazetted** to share buildings with one another.

Although **guidelines** to this Act have been revised a number of times the Act itself remains substantially unaltered and there are no plans to revise it.

APPROPRIATE AUTHORITIES

By the appropriate authorities is meant those required under the **Act** to be designated as those responsible (a) for determining who the **parties** to a particular **Sharing Agreement** should be, and whose **consent** shall be required for it; and (b) for keeping a register of such Sharing Agreements. The appropriate authority under which a local **congregation** falls depends upon its **denominational** polity. Because of the likely differences between the congregations involved in a **Sharing Agreement** sensitivity is needed concerning the ways in which the "other" church(es) work(s). Each must abide by the authority appropriate to its tradition.

BUILDINGS

Sharing Agreements under the **Act** are possible with regard to new or existing church buildings, including church halls, youth clubs and residences for ministers, clergy and lay workers. With certain exceptions (see **Peculiars**) the Act makes provision for **Sharing Agreements** in respect of church buildings throughout **England/Wales.**

CANONS B43 and B44

Along with the Church of England (Ecumenical Relations) Measure 1988 these canons provide legal authority for certain types of ecumenical co-operation involving the Church of England (see page 4).

CHURCH/DENOMINATION/TRADITION/UNION

Some church traditions properly refer to themselves as a **denomination** rather than as a **church.** This is especially the case where church polity is of congregational government but where such congregations have freely joined a **union** of like-minded fellowships. In this publication both church and denomination are used as roughly interchangeable, since the context makes clear whether the reference is to a local **congregation** or to a wider body. Sometimes it is sufficient to refer to a particular **tradition.** Other works must be consulted for details of the variety of church government.

CONGREGATION

A **congregation** is to be distinguished from the understanding of **church** (as used above), even though in some cases it may be the same body. A **Sharing Agreement** normally affects two or more local congregations, whatever differences there may be in church polity. A **congregation** comprises those Christians formed into a worshipping fellowship in a particular location who may find that it is desirable for them to come "Under the Same Roof" as another such local congregation. Some of these congregations will have authority vested in themselves, subject to a **Trust Deed**, permitting them to make appropriate decisions regarding a **Sharing Agreement**. Others will be subject to a different **appropriate authority** within their particular denomination.

CONSENTS

Those whose approval must formally be obtained according to the **church's** polity before the **Sharing Agreement** can be signed are listed in chapter 12 of this booklet.

COUNCIL OF CHURCHES FOR BRITAIN AND IRELAND

The constitution of the **Council of Churches for Britain and Ireland,** which was inaugurated in 1990, explicitly states that it is the legal successor to the British Council of Churches, through which body, for the purpose of the 1969 **Act** (alongside the Evangelical Alliance and the British Evangelical Council) earlier applications for **gazetting** of churches were made. It is thus through the **CCBI** (or through one of the other two continuing bodies above) that future gazetting should be arranged (see pages 2-4).

DENOMINATION
See **Church** above.

ECUMENICAL COUNCIL
A body appointed in accordance with the Constitution of the **Local Ecumenical Project** to oversee the day to day life of the project, and having certain responsibilities that would normally be exercised in a single **denomination** situation by the Parochial Church Council, Church Council or Church Meeting.

ENCYCLOPAEDIA OF FORMS AND PRECEDENTS
A reference book to which every solicitor has access and which contains precedents for **Sharing Agreements**, which do not therefore have to be drawn up from scratch each time.

ENGLAND/WALES
The law to which the 1969 Act relates applies to England and Wales. Jersey and the Isle of Man have been brought under its provisions but no such legislation exists for Scotland, Ireland or Guernsey. The Church of England has a special place within this law as the Established Church and, for the most part in these **guidelines** is to be distinguished from the Church in Wales (which became disestablished in 1920) and all other **churches** referred to. There are, however, similarities between the Church of England and the Church in Wales with regard to marriage laws and **Faculty Jurisdiction.**

EXECUTION
Where previously legal agreements were referred to upon completion as being "signed and sealed" the common term now used is for them to be "executed", that is, become binding.

FACULTY JURISDICTION
The legal requirements relating to the fabric, ornaments and furniture of Church of England churches, which place obligations on the incumbent and the parochial church council for upkeep and care and specify what permission needs to be sought for alterations.

GAZETTING

Publication in the *London Gazette* of **churches** wishing to be in a position to avail themselves of the provisions of the **1969 Act** (see pages 3-4). Gazetting is normally done by a **denomination** or federation of churches to cover all churches (congregations) in its membership. Those currently within the terms of the Act are listed in chapter 12, with appropriate references.

"GUEST" CONGREGATION

The **congregation(s)** permitted by a **Sharing Agreement** to use the **building** in question to all intents and purposes as if it was its own – that is, to practise the rites and procedures of its own **tradition** – except that the **"guest"** congregation may not dispose of any part of the building or contents or otherwise prevent the continuing use of it by the **"host"** congregation.

GUIDELINES

The present booklet tries to set out in a practical commentary how the **1969 Act** may be used as the basis for a **Sharing Agreement.** These **guidelines** must not be seen as in any way amending or contravening the Act. Other publications are referred to which set out possibilities for **churches** not wishing to enter into a formal agreement under the **Act.**

"HOST"/"OWNING" CONGREGATION

The **congregation** of the **church** to which the building in question legally belongs, and which enters into a **Sharing Agreement** permitting (an)other congregation(s) to enjoy the use of the **building** as if it belonged to them (see **"Guest" Congregation**).

JOINT COUNCIL

A council representing the sharing **churches** which, whilst not strictly necessary in the terms of the **Act,** is highly desirable for the smooth running of the **Sharing Agreement** (see chapter 6).

LEGAL CHARGE

A **Legal Charge** is a mortgage. Its purpose is to give protection to a **"guest"** congregation in respect of a substantial capital contribution towards the cost of rebuilding, extension or refurbishment of a building owned by a **"host"** congregation. The **Legal Charge,** which is made on the building in the **Sharing Agreement** itself or in a separate document, ensures that if the agreement is **terminated,** capital contributed is returned to the contributor in the way specified in the Charge. The Charge may be for a fixed sum of money but is more usually for a percentage of eventual net sale proceeds with the sum or share charged being payable at the time when the building is sold. The **Legal Charge** cannot be made to apply to a consecrated Church of England building (see chapter 9).

LOCAL ECUMENICAL PROJECTS

A **Local Ecumenical Project** (LEP) is the term currently used "where there is at the level of the local church a formal, written agreement affecting the ministry, congregational life and/or buildings of more than one denomination; and a recognition of that agreement by appropriate denominational authorities" (see page 2). There are currently over 700 such LEPs in England and more than 60 in Wales.

MODEL AGREEMENTS

Some typical **Sharing Agreements** are set out as examples in Appendix II. By referring to these or others readily obtainable by application to appropriate **denominational** headquarters a great deal of unnecessary work and mistakes can be avoided.

"OWNING" CONGREGATION

See "Host" Congregation.

PARTIES

Parties are those actually signing the **Sharing Agreement.** They are listed in chapter 12.

PASTORAL MEASURE

The **Pastoral Measure, 1983,** replaces the **Pastoral Measure, 1968,** referred to in the **Act.** Under this Measure, which relates to the Church of England, pastoral schemes may be drawn up. These may provide for the licensing of buildings for public worship according to the rites of the Church of England and may also enable joint ownership of church buildings by the Church of England and another **church** or churches. Other matters for which pastoral schemes are required are alterations to parish boundaries and the formation of team or group ministries.

PECULIARS

A **Peculiar** means a place of worship which is exempt from the jurisdiction of the bishop of the diocese and therefore from the **Faculty Jurisdiction. Peculiars** along with extra-diocesan and extra-parochial churches of the Church of England may not enter into a **Sharing Agreement** under this Act (see page 4).

SHARING AGREEMENT

In order to apply the **1969 Act** a formal agreement has to be entered into on behalf of the **congregations** concerned. All the implications of this are set out in chapters 2 to 11, and form the main subject of these **guidelines.**

SPONSORING BODY

An ecumenical body, usually at county level, representative of the **denominations** involved in a **Local Ecumenical Project** and responsible for overseeing the project. Its functions are usually now included in those of Intermediate/County bodies in England.

TERMINATION

The way in which a **Sharing Agreement** may be ended is dealt with in chapter 9.

TRADITION

See **Church** above.

TRUST DEED

The legal foundation deed, which sets out what is permitted within a given building (often qualified by the use of the term "normally" or "occasionally").

TRUSTEES

A **Trust Deed** is safeguarded by a body of continuing **trustees,** either private individuals replaced as becomes necessary through death or resignation or – becoming more frequently the case – by a Trust Corporation.

UNIFIED CHURCH

Churches which have merged their former identities into a common constitution may be said to be unified. However, it should be noted that a **Sharing Agreement** DOES NOT constitute a **unified church** (see chapter 5).

UNION

See **Church** above.

WALES

See **England/Wales** above for differences/similarities between the Church of England and the Church in Wales.

Appendix II
Simple Sharing Agreements
(a) Methodist/Another Church on
Methodist premises

INFORMATION TO BE SUPPLIED

The Property Division will need information on the following points in order to be able to produce a draft of any particular Sharing Agreement: the numbers relate to those shown (*n) in the text:

1. The names of two members of the Methodist Church Council (MCC) who have been authorised under Section 82 of the Charities Act 1993 to sign.
2. The name of the MCC.
3. The collective address for service of the MCC, which could be that of the Superintendent Minister or a lay officer of the MCC.
4. The full names of any individuals to be party to the Agreement on behalf of the guest church together with the offices they hold.
5. The address of 4. above.
6. The correct description of any corporate body to be party to the Agreement on behalf of the guest church.
7. The address of 6. above.
8. The name of the guest church.
9. Recital 5(b): authority for the guest church parties.
10. Recital 6(b): any consents required by the guest church to this Agreement.
11. Cl 3(2): the person/body who would authorise a resolution by the Joint Council (JC) on behalf of the guest church.
12. Clauses 4(4) and 4(5): the person/body who will accept responsibility for the guest church's share of the common costs of management.
13. Cl 6(3): the person/body who would approve capital contributions on behalf of the guest church.
14. Cl 9: the person/body who will give consent to joint services on behalf of the guest church.
15. Cl 10(3): the person/body to whom notice would be given to terminate the Agreement on behalf of the guest church.

16. Cl 10(4): the person/body who would give notice to terminate the Agreement on behalf of the guest church.
17. Cl 10(4): the person/body whose consent is required for notice to be given to terminate by the guest church.
18. Cl 11(b): any definitions required by the guest church.
19. Cl 11(c): any offices or bodies of the guest church to be referred to.
20. First Schedule: details required to complete the description of the property to be shared. The Land Registry title number of the property is not essential and so would only be included where it is known already or can be discovered without difficulty.
21. Second Schedule Cl 3: the members of the JC on behalf of the guest church: names of offices rather than office-holders are required, and (where appropriate) the means by which persons will be elected or appointed.
22. The correct wording of the attestation clause required for any corporate body party to the Agreement on behalf of the guest church.
23. The person/body required to register the Agreement on behalf of the guest church pursuant to Section 1(8) of the Sharing of Church Buildings Act 1969.
24. The address of the property to be shared, for the cover.

The Division is happy to correspond direct with the appropriate officers of the guest church in respect of points 4-19 and 21-23.

The Division has separate editions of this standard form and information sheet for use where the guest church is either **the Church of England** or **the United Reformed Church.**

The Methodist Church Property Division   October 1993
Central Buildings
Oldham Street
Manchester M1 1JQ
T.N. 061-236-5194
FAX: 061-236-0752

SHARING AGREEMENT

This **SHARING AGREEMENT** is made the_____day of_____19___
between THE TRUSTEES FOR METHODIST CHURCH PURPOSES of
Central Buildings Oldham Street Manchester M1 1JQ (hereinafter called
"the Board") being a charitable body corporate established by the
Methodist Church Act 1939 of the first part_____(*1)
and_____(*1) and others the members or such of the members as
have attained full age of_____(*2) METHODIST CHURCH
COUNCIL (hereinafter called "the Methodist Church Council") whose
collective address for service is _____
_____ (*3)
of the second part the Reverend _____being the
Secretary of the Methodist Church Committee known as "the Committee
for Local Ecumenical Development" (hereinafter called "the Policy
Committee") of 1 Central Buildings Westminster London SW1H 9NH of
the third part   (*4)
of_____(*5) of the fourth part (and_____(*6)
whose registered office address is situate at_____(*7)
of the fifth part)

WHEREAS
1.   The Sharing of Church Buildings Act 1969 (hereinafter called "the
     1969 Act") has made provision for the making of Sharing
     Agreements between (among other Churches) the Methodist
     Church and the_____(*8) Church for the sharing by them
     of Church Buildings (such Churches being hereinafter called "the
     two Churches")

2.   The two Churches wish to make a Sharing Agreement pursuant to
     the 1969 Act for sharing the building (hereinafter called "the
     Church Building") more particularly described in the First Schedule
     hereto

3.   All the parties hereto have agreed to enter into this Deed upon the
     terms hereinafter appearing in order to fulfil that wish

4.   The Church Building is vested in the Methodist Board as custodian
     trustees upon the model trusts of the Methodist Church for the time
     being contained in Part III of Schedule 2 to the Methodist Church
     Act 1976 and in accordance with Part II of Schedule 2 to the said
     Act the management of the Church Building and the exercise of
     any power or discretion expressed to be exercisable by the trustees

41

or the managing trustees under the said model trusts are vested in the Methodist Church Council

5.   Pursuant to Section 1(3) of the 1969 Act

(a) The Board the Methodist Church Council and the Secretary of the Policy Committee are the persons or bodies determined by the Annual Conference of the Methodist Church as proper parties to execute as respects the Methodist Church a Sharing Agreement relating to the Church Building

(b) _____ (*9)

6.   Pursuant to Section 1(4) of the 1969 Act

(a) The consent of the Board of the Property Division of the Methodist Church (hereinafter called "the Property Division") has been obtained

(b) The consent(s) of _____(*10) have been obtained

7.   This Agreement has been approved and ordered to be executed by a resolution passed by a duly constituted meeting of the Methodist Church Council and is intended to be executed by two members of the Methodist Church Council upon whom the Methodist Church Council acting under Section 82 of the Charities Act 1993 has conferred authority

NOW THIS DEED made pursuant to the powers given by the 1969 Act WITNESSETH AND IT IS HEREBY AGREED AND DECLARED as follows

1. ____ THE Church Building shall remain vested as heretofore but the purposes for which it is applicable shall include the purpose and provisions of this Agreement

2. ____ THERE shall be a Joint Council of the two Churches constituted in accordance with the provisions of the Second Schedule hereto for the following purposes

(a) To settle any questions that may arise regarding the times at which the two Churches are to have the use of the Church Building

(b) To advise those responsible for the maintenance and repair of the Church Building on behalf of the congregations of the two Churches regarding financial questions and particularly regarding any exceptional expenditure

(c) To organise or to consider and if thought fit to approve proposals for the raising of such common funds as are to be raised by the congregations of the two Churches acting together and

(d) Generally to facilitate joint action and the settlement of questions of detail which may arise in the carrying out of this Agreement

3.   (1) THE two Churches shall be regarded in principle as having equal rights to the use of the Church Building and as being equally responsible for meeting the cost of management but if the Joint Council shall for any reason be of the opinion that some proportion other than equality be adopted then some other proportion may from time to time be agreed by the Joint Council as representing

(a) The proportion in which in principle the two Churches are entitled to use the Church Building and

(b) The proportion in which they are responsible for the cost of management

but so that the two proportions need not necessarily be the same

(2) Any such Agreement shall be effected by a resolution of the Joint Council made with the consent of the Superintendent Minister and the Property Division on behalf of the Methodist Church and with the consent of_____(*11) on behalf of the_____(*8) Church

(3) In this Agreement the "agreed proportion" means equality or such proportion other than equality as may at the time have been agreed under this Clause

4.   (1) THE responsibility for the management of the Church Building shall remain in the body (hereinafter called "the responsible authority") responsible therefor immediately before the execution of this Agreement but in the future discharge of that responsibility the provisions of this Clause shall apply

43

(2) The responsible authority shall generally consult the Joint Council on questions of policy regarding expenditure on management and except in cases of emergency shall consult that Council before incurring unusual expenditure

(3) The following shall be regarded as common costs of management namely

(a) Rent mortgage interest insurance fiscal liabilities and other outgoings which are normally charged against income
(b) The cost of repair of the Church Building and when necessary the replacement of fixtures and other furnishings goods and ornaments thereof (provided that this provision shall not extend to the cost of structural repairs to the main walls roof or foundations) and
(c) The cost of upkeep including heating lighting cleaning and caretaking and the provision of necessary amenities other than amenities (such as books for use in a particular form of service) which are peculiar to one or other of the two Churches

(4)   So far as the same are not met out of funds raised as common funds it shall be the responsibility of the Methodist Church Council and_____(*12) to provide in the agreed proportion the common costs of management and to reimburse the responsible authority accordingly

(5)   If the sharing of the Church Building shall be terminated by notice under Clause 10 an Account shall be prepared of the sums to be provided under this Clause up to the date of expiry of the notice all necessary apportionments being made as at that date and the Methodist Church Council and_____(*12) shall be responsible for providing in the agreed proportion the sum found due on each Account as soon as the same shall be ascertained

5. ____ THE responsible authority shall not incur substantial capital expenditure on the improvement of the Church Building without first consulting the Joint Council

6. ____ (1) FOR the improvement of the Church Building or for any purpose for which a capital sum is required in connection with the Church Building the responsible authority may with the consent of the Joint Council accept money from any person on the footing

that it is to be regarded as a capital contribution made by the one or the other of the two Churches under this Clause

(2) Such a capital contribution shall be spent for improvement or other capital purposes for which it is given and may be accepted on such terms as to repayment and otherwise as the responsible authority shall authorise

(3) The responsible authority shall not accept any such capital contribution on any terms which have not been previously approved in writing by the Property Division on behalf of the Methodist Church and by_____(*13) on behalf of the _____(*8) Church

7._____THE Church Building shall be made available for worship in accordance with the forms of service and practice of each of the two Churches and the extent to which it shall be available for and the particular times at which it shall be used for the one form of service or the other shall be determined from time to time by the Joint Council guided for that purpose by the principle stated in Clause 3

8._____AN INVITATION may be given to a minister or lay preacher of either of the two Churches to take part in conducting worship in the Church Building in accordance with the forms of service and practice of the inviting Church and such invitation may be accepted PROVIDED that in giving accepting or carrying into effect such invitation the persons concerned shall comply with any rules and directions in that behalf of each of the two Churches

9._____SUBJECT to compliance with any rules or directions given in that behalf by either of the two Churches joint services may be held in the Church Building on such occasions as may be agreed between the Superintendent Minister and_____(*14)

10._____(1) EITHER of the two Churches may by notice given under this Clause bring to an end the sharing of the Church Building

(2) From the expiry of such notice the Church Building shall be held on the trusts or for the purposes on or for which it was held immediately before the execution of this Agreement and this Agreement shall cease to have effect for the purpose of settling accounts between the two Churches

(3) Notice under this Clause by the Methodist Church shall be a notice in writing signed by or on behalf of the Secretary of the Policy Committee given with the consent of the Property Division to_____(*15)

(4) Notice under this Clause by the_____(*8) Church shall be a notice in writing signed by or on behalf of_____(*16) given with the consent of _____ (*17) to the Secretary of the Policy Committee

(5) No notice given under this Clause shall be for less than six months unless the persons to whom it is to be given agree to accept shorter notice

11.___ IN THIS Agreement save when the context otherwise requires

    (a) "The Superintendent Minister" means the Superintendent Minister of the Circuit of the Methodist Church in which the Church Building is for the time being situate

    (b) _____ (*18)

    (c) Reference to the Superintendent Minister the Property Division of the Methodist Church Council the Secretary of the Policy Committee_____(*19) includes a reference to the person or body who by reason of any vacancy of office or any change in the constitution of the Methodist Church and/or the_____(*8) Church is for the time being charged with the responsibilities of the person or body named

IN WITNESS whereof the Board (and_____(*6)) (has hereunto caused its/have hereunto caused their respective) Common Seal(s) to be affixed and_____(*1) and_____(*1) and the Reverend _____and_____(*4) have hereunto set their respective hands the day and year first hereinbefore written

THE FIRST SCHEDULE hereto

ALL THAT piece or parcel of land situate at_____ _____(*20) in_____(*20) TOGETHER WITH the buildings erected thereon or on some part thereof and known as _____ (*20) as the same is registered at HM Land Registry under Title Number_____(*20)

46

THE SECOND SCHEDULE hereto

Constitution of the Joint Council

1. The Joint Council shall consist of an equal number of members of each of the two Churches which number shall be six or such other number as the Joint Council shall from time to time determine

2. The members of the Joint Council who are members of the Methodist Church shall consist of

    (a) The Superintendent Minister and the Minister with pastoral charge at the Church Building if a Methodist Minister who shall be ex-officio members
    (b) Four persons (or such other number of persons as may be required to complete the number of members of the Joint Council who are members of the Methodist Church) elected annually by the Methodist Church Council

3. The members of the Joint Council who are members of the _____ (*8) Church shall consist of _____ _____ (*21)

4. Ex-officio members may each appoint a deputy either generally or for a particular meeting to act in their place at a meeting when they are not present in person and such members present by deputy shall be deemed to be present at a meeting and their deputies may at the meeting exercise all the rights which they might have exercised

5. Members to be elected at an annual meeting shall hold office until the next annual meeting of the body which elected them and shall be eligible for re-election but if then no persons shall be elected in their places (unless otherwise expressly resolved by the body which elects them) they shall be deemed to have been re-elected for a further year

6. (a) The Superintendent Minister or his/her deputy shall be Chairman of the Joint Council
    (b) When the Chairman is not available to take the chair those present shall choose one of their number to be Chairman for that meeting

7. The quorum at a meeting shall be four or such other number as the Joint Council may from time to time decide but so that no meeting shall be deemed to have a quorum unless at least one member of each of the two Churches is present

8. Every matter shall be determined by the majority of the members of the Joint Council present and voting on the question provided that in case of equality of votes the Chairman shall have a second or casting vote

9. A casual vacancy in the Joint Council shall not invalidate its proceedings

10. Subject to the foregoing provisions of this Schedule the Joint Council shall from time to time regulate its own procedure and shall cause minutes to be kept of all its meetings

THE COMMON SEAL of THE   )
TRUSTEES FOR METHODIST   )
CHURCH PURPOSES was   )
hereunto affixed with the sanction   )
of the two Trustees whose   )
signatures are hereunto subscribed   )   CS

SIGNED as a DEED and   )
DELIVERED by the said _____   )
(*1) in the presence of   ) _____

SIGNED as a DEED and   )
DELIVERED by the said _____   )
(*1) in the presence of   ) _____

SIGNED as a DEED and   )
DELIVERED by the said   )

_____   )

in the presence of   ) _____

THE COMMON SEAL of _____
_____ (*6)   )
was hereunto affixed   )
_____ (*22)   )
)   CS

SIGNED as a DEED and
DELIVERED by the said _____   )
(*4) in the presence of   )
) _____

SIGNED as a DEED and
DELIVERED by the said _____   )
(*4) in the presence of   ) _____

48

SA_____REGISTERED
by THE METHODIST BOARD
OF PROPERTY on behalf of THE
METHODIST CHURCH this
day of_____ 19 _____
Secretary
_____

REGISTERED by_____
_____(*23) on
behalf of THE _____
_____ (*8) CHURCH

METHODIST/OTHER
<u>METHODIST owned CHAPEL</u>

DATED _____ 19___

THE TRUSTEES FOR
METHODIST CHURCH
PURPOSES
AND OTHERS

and

_____ (*6)

AND

_____ (*4)

SHARING AGREEMENT

relating to

_____(*23)

(b) Church of England/
Shiloh Church on Church of England premises

DRAFT SHARING AGREEMENT

THIS SHARING AGREEMENT is made the_____day of _____One
thousand nine hundred and ninety_____BETWEEN_____DIOCESAN
BOARD OF FINANCE whose registered office is situate at
_____(being the Diocesan Authority of the Diocese of
_____for the purpose of the Parochial Church Councils
(Powers) Measure 1956 and the Diocesan Board of Finance for the Diocese
for the purposes of the Act hereinafter mentioned) (hereinafter called "the
Board") of the first part THE PAROCIAL CHURCH COUNCIL OF THE
ECCLESIASTICAL PARISH OF_____

in the City and Diocese of_____(hereinafter called "the Parochial
Church Council") of the second part THE REVEREND_____Clerk
in Holy Orders _____ of _____
in the City and Diocese of _____(hereinafter called "the
Incumbent") of the third part THE NATIONAL/INTERNATIONAL
COORDINATOR OF THE SHILOH UNITED CHURCH OF CHRIST
APOSTOLIC (WORLDWIDE) of_____(hereinafter
called "the Shiloh Church") of the fourth part and THE REVEREND
_____PASTOR OF THE SHILOH UNITED CHURCH OF
CHRIST APOSTOLIC (WORLDWIDE) (_____BRANCH)
of the fifth part

WHEREAS
1.   The Sharing of Church Buildings Act 1969 (hereinafter called "the
       1969 Act") has made provision for the making of Sharing
       Agreements between (amongst other churches) The Church of
       England and the Shiloh Church for the sharing by them of church
       buildings (such churches being hereinafter called "the two
       Churches")

2. The two Churches wish to make a Sharing Agreement pursuant to the 1969 Act for sharing the building (hereinafter called "the Church Building") more particularly described in the First Schedule hereto

3. The Church Building is vested in the Board as the Diocesan Authority of the said diocese in accordance with Section 6 of the Parochial Church Councils (Powers) Measure 1956 upon trust for the Parochial Church Council for such of the purposes specified in Section 5 of the said measure as are charitable

4. The Board the Parochial Church Council and the Incumbent being the proper parties as regards the Church of England to be made parties hereto under Section 1 (3) of the 1969 Act have agreed with the Shiloh Church being a proper party as regards the Shiloh Church to be made parties hereto under the 1969 Act to enter into this deed upon the terms hereinafter appearing in order to fulfil such wish

NOW THIS DEED MADE PURSUANT TO THE POWERS GIVEN BY THE 1969 ACT WITNESSETH AND IT IS HEREBY AGREED AND DECLARED AS FOLLOWS

1. ___THE Church Building shall remain vested as heretofor but the purposes for which it is applicable shall include the purpose and provisions of this Agreement

2. ___THERE shall be a joint Council of the two Churches constituted in accordance with the provisions of the Second Schedule for the following purposes

    (a) to settle any questions that may arise regarding the times at which the two Churches are to have the use of the Church Building

    (b) to advise those responsible for the maintenance and repair of the Church Building on behalf of the congregations of the two Churches regarding financial questions and particularly regarding any exceptional expenditure

    (c) to organise or consider and if thought fit to approve proposals for the raising of such common funds as are to be jointly raised by the congregations acting together and

    (d) generally to facilitate joint action and the settlement of questions of detail which may arise in the carrying out of this agreement

3.   (1) THE two Churches shall be regarded in principal as having equal rights to the use of the Church Building and as being equally responsible for meeting the cost of management subject to the provisions of clause 4 (4) hereof but if the Joint Council shall for any reason be of the opinion that some proportion other than equality be adopted then some other proportion may from time to time be agreed by the Joint Council as representing

(a) the proportion in which in principal the two Churches are entitled to use the Church Building and
(b) the proportion in which they are responsible for the cost of management and so that the two proportions need not necessarily be the same

(2) any such agreement shall be effected by a resolution of the Joint Council made with the consent of the Parochial Church Council on behalf of the Church of England and with the consent of the Shiloh Church

(3) in this Agreement the "Agreed Proportion" means equality or such other proportion other than equality as may from time to time have been agreed under this clause

4.   (1) THE ultimate responsibility for the management of the Church Building shall remain in the Parochial Church Council (hereinafter called "the Responsible Authority") but in the future discharge of that responsibility the provisions of this clause shall apply

(2) the Responsible Authority shall generally consult the Joint Council on questions of policy regarding expenditure on management and except in cases of emergency shall consult that Council before incurring unusual expenditure.

(3) the following shall be regarded as costs of management namely

(a) rent mortgage interest insurance fiscal liabilities and other outgoings which are normally charged against income
(b) the cost of repair of the Church Building and when necessary of

fixtures and other furnishings goods and ornaments thereof (provided that this provision shall not extend to the cost of structural repairs to the main roofs wall or foundations) and

(c) the costs of upkeep including heating lighting cleaning and caretaking and the provision of necessary amenities other than amenities (such as books for use in a particular type of service) which are peculiar to any of the two Churches

(4) so far as the same are not met out of the funds raised as common funds it shall be the responsibility of the two local Churches to provide in the agreed proportion the common costs of management and to reimburse the Responsible Authority accordingly

(5) if the sharing of the Church Building shall be terminated by notice under clause 10 accounts shall be prepared of the sums to be provided under this clause up to the date of expiry of the notice all necessary apportionments being made as at that date and the two Churches shall be responsible for providing in the agreed proportion the sum found due on each account as soon as the same shall be ascertained

5.   THE Responsible Authority shall not incur substantial capital expenditure on the improvement of the Church Building without first consulting the Joint Council

6.   (1) FOR the improvement of the Church Building or for any other purpose for which a capital sum is required in connection with the Church Building the Responsible Authority may with the consent of the Joint Council accept money from any person on the footing that it is to be regarded as a capital contribution made by the other of the two Churches under this clause

(2) such capital contribution shall be spent for the improvement or other capital purposes for which it is given and may be accepted on such terms as to repayment and otherwise as the Responsible Authority shall authorise

(3) The Responsible Authority shall not accept any such capital contribution on any terms which have not been previously approved in writing by the Board and the Parochial Church Council on behalf of the Church of England and by the Shiloh Church

7. THE Church Building shall be made available for worship in accordance with the forms of service and practice of each of the two Churches and the extent to which it shall be available for and the particular times at which it shall be used for any one form of service shall be determined from time to time by the Joint Council guided for that purpose by the principle stated in clause 3.

8. A Minister Reader or Lay Preacher of either of the two Churches may invite a Minister Reader or Lay Preacher of the other of the two Churches to take part in conducting worship in the Church Building in accordance with the forms of service and the practice of the inviting church and such invitation may be accepted PROVIDED that in giving accepting or carrying into effect such invitation the persons concerned shall comply with any rules and directions in that behalf of each of the two Churches

9. SUBJECT to compliance with any rules or directions given in that behalf by either of the two Churches joint services may be held in the Church Building on such occasions as may be agreed between the Incumbent and the Minister of the Shiloh congregation

10. (1) EITHER of the two Churches may by notice given under this clause bring to an end the sharing of the Church Building

(2) from the expiry of such notice the Church Building shall be held on the trusts and for the purposes on or for which it was held immediately before the execution of this Agreement and this Agreement shall cease to have effect except for the purpose of settling accounts between the two Churches

(3) notice under this clause by the Church of England shall be a notice in writing signed by or on behalf of the Incumbent given with the consent of the Bishop to the Pastor of the Shiloh Church (_____branch and to the National/International Coordinator of the Shiloh Church)

(4) notice under this clause by the Shiloh Church shall be a notice in writing signed by or on behalf of the Pastor of the Shiloh Church given with the consent of its local Church Meeting and of the

National/International Coordinator of the Shiloh Church to the Incumbent but should the number of Shiloh Church members fall below three any notice shall be given by or on behalf of the National Executive Board of the Shiloh Church to the Incumbent

(5) no notice given under this clause shall be for less than six months unless the persons to whom it is given agree to accept shorter notice

11.   IN this Agreement save where the context otherwise requires

    (a) reference to the Shiloh National Executive Board and the National/International Coordinator of the Shiloh Church includes a reference to the person or body who by reason of any vacancy or office or any change in the constitution of the Shiloh Church is for the time being charged with the responsibilities of the person or body named

    (b) reference to the Bishop means the Bishop for the time being of the Diocese of _____

IN WITNESS whereof the_____Diocesan Board of Finance and the Shiloh Church have caused their respective Common Seals to be hereunto affixed and the Reverend_____as Chairman presiding and _____
_____ and _____
(two other members of the Parochial Church Council present at a meeting of the Council held on the _____ day of _____
199____ at which a resolution was passed authorising the execution of this deed) or have on behalf of the Parochial Church Council hereunto set their respective hands and the Incumbent has hereunto set his hand the day and year first hereinbefore written

THE FIRST SCHEDULE

ALL THAT piece of land situate_____in the City of _____ with the building known as _____
_____ erected thereon

THE SECOND SCHEDULE

Constitution of the Joint Council

1. The Joint Council shall consist of an equal number of members of each of the two Churches which number shall be five or such other number as the Joint Council shall from time to time determine

2. The members of the Joint Council who are members of the Church of England shall be
    (a) the Incumbent who shall be an ex officio member
    (b) such other number of persons as shall be required to complete the number of members of the Joint Council who are members of the Church of England as the Parochial Church Council shall from time to time appoint and so that members so appointed shall hold office for so long as that Council shall determine

3. The members of the Joint Council who are members of the Shiloh Church shall consist of the Minister of the Shiloh Church and four persons to be elected by the Shiloh Church and four persons to be elected by the Shiloh Church (_____branch) Church Meeting and the members so elected shall hold office so long as that meeting shall determine

4. (i)   the Incumbent shall be the Chairman of the Joint Council
    (ii)   during a vacancy in the said benefice the Rural Dean shall take the place of the Incumbent as a member of the Joint Council and shall act as Chairman
    (iii) should the Chairman not be available to take the chair for any meeting then those present shall choose one of their number to be Chairman for that meeting

5. An ex officio member may appoint a Deputy either generally or for a particular meeting to act in his place at a meeting when he is not present in person and such a member present by Deputy shall be deemed to be present at a meeting and his Deputy may at the meeting exercise all the rights which he might have exercised

6. A member to be elected at an annual meeting shall hold office until the next annual meeting of the body which elected him and shall be eligible for re-election but if then no person shall be elected in his place (unless otherwise expressly resolved by the body which elects him) he shall be deemed to have been re-elected for a further year

7. The quorum at a meeting shall be five or such other number as the Joint Council may from time to time decide but so that no meeting shall be deemed to have a quorum unless at least one representative of each of the two Churches is present

8. Every matter shall be determined by the majority of the members of the Joint Council present and voting on the question provided that in case of equality of votes the Chairman of the meeting shall have a second or casting vote

9. A casual vacancy of the membership of the Joint Council shall not invalidate its proceedings

10 Subject to the foregoing provisions of this Schedule the Joint Council may from time to time regulate its own procedure

EXECUTED (but not delivered)
until the date hereof) by)
affixing THE COMMON SEAL)
of THE_____DIOCESAN)
BOARD OF FINANCE in the)
presence of)

        Two members of the Council

        Deputy Secretary

EXECUTED (but not delivered)   SIGNED AS A DEED AND)
until the date hereof) by)   DELIVERED by the said _____)
affixing THE COMMON SEAL)   _____ (as the Incumbent))
of THE SHILOH UNITED)   in the presence of)
CHURCH OF CHRIST)
APOSTOLIC (WORLDWIDE))
in the presence of)   SIGNED AS A DEED AND)
  DELIVERED by the said)
  REVEREND _____)
SIGNED AS A DEED AND)   on behalf of the Shiloh United)
DELIVERED by the said)   Church of Christ Apostolic)
REVEREND _____)   (Worldwide) (_____Branch))
and _____)   (as the local Pastor) in the)
and)   presence of)
on behalf of the Parochial)
Church Council in the presence)
of)

Appendix III

Sharing of Church Buildings Act 1969
Revised to 1st December 1977

© Crown copyright 1978: reproduced by permission of HMSO

ARRANGEMENT OF SECTIONS

An Act to provide for the sharing and using of church buildings by different Churches and for matters connected therewith. [25th July 1969]

1. – (1) It shall be lawful, notwithstanding any statutory or other legal provision, for any two or more Churches to which this Act applies to make agreements, through the parties mentioned in this section and in accordance with the provisions thereof, for the sharing by them of church buildings, and to carry such agreements into effect, and such agreements are in this Act referred to as "sharing agreements".

Agreements for sharing church buildings.

(2) A sharing agreement may be made in respect of a single church building or two or more church buildings in the same locality, and in respect of any existing or proposed church building, and, subject to the following provisions of this Act relating to consecrated churches of the Church of England and the sharing of residential buildings, may provide for the shared building or any of the shared buildings to be owned or continue to be owned by one only of the sharing Churches or to be jointly owned by all or some of the sharing Churches.

(3)   The parties to a sharing agreement shall –
  (a) as respects the Church of England, be the Diocesan Board of Finance of the diocese and the incumbent and parochial church council of the parish in which the building or buildings is or are or will be situated;*
  (b) as respects any other Church, be such persons as may be determined by the appropriate authority of that Church;

and shall also include, in the case of an existing building, the person (if not otherwise a party) in whom the building is vested and any managing trustees thereof, and may also include, in the case of a proposed building, any person in whom it is to be vested or who is to be a managing trustee thereof.

(4) A sharing agreement shall not be made on behalf of the Church of England without the consent of the bishop and the Pastoral Committee of the diocese concerned, and the

---

* On February 22nd 1994 the General Synod of the Church of England gave final approval to the Teams and Group Ministries Measure which would insert the following clause at this point in the Sharing of Church Buildings Act, 1969:

"and, where a team ministry is established for the benefice comprising that parish, –
  (i) any vicar in the team ministry to whom a special cure of souls in respect of the parish has been assigned by a scheme under the Pastoral Measure 1983 or by his licence from the bishop; or
  (ii) any member of the team to whom a special responsibility for pastoral care in respect of the parish has been assigned under section 20(8A) of that Measure, the parish not being one in respect of which a special cure of souls has been assigned as mentioned in paragraph (i) above"

However, at the time of going to press the Measure has not been approved by either House of Parliament or received the Royal Assent. Further information about the date at which the Measure will come into force is obtainable from the General Synod Office, Church House, Great Smith Street, London SW1P 3NZ.

appropriate authority of any other Church to which this Act applies may require the consent of any body or person specified by the authority to be given to sharing agreements made on behalf of that Church.

(5) Where a church building is held on trust for educational purposes which include instruction in religious knowledge according to the faith and practice of the Church of England, the consent of the Diocesan Education Committee of the diocese concerned to a sharing agreement in respect of that building shall be required in lieu of the consent of the Pastoral Committee thereof, and the agreement shall be subject to the approval of the Secretary of State.

1968 No. 1.

(6) Where a benefice is vacant and a suspension period is current under section 67 of the Pastoral Measure 1968, subsection (3)(a) of this section shall have effect with the substitution for the reference to the incumbent of a reference to the minister in charge of the parish, but otherwise a sharing agreement shall not be made on behalf of the Church of England during a vacancy in the benefice concerned.

(7) Where a see is vacant, or the bishop of the diocese is unable because of illness or absence to give his consent under subsection (4) of this section, the archbishop of the province may appoint by an instrument under his hand a suffragan or assistant bishop or an archdeacon of the diocese to act in place of the bishop under the said subsection for a period specified in the instrument; and in the event of a vacancy in the see of an archbishop or his illness or absence, an appointment under this subsection, either in respect of the see of the archbishop or another see in the province, may be made by the other archbishop.

(8) A sharing agreement shall be under seal and shall be registered, in the case of the Church of England, in the registries of the province and diocese, and, in the case of other Churches, in the registry or office of the appropriate authority, and the consents required as aforesaid shall be signified in writing by the secretary or clerk of the body concerned or by the person concerned and shall be registered with the deed.

(9) A sharing agreement shall be binding on the successors to the parties thereto, that is to say, on the persons who would at any subsequent time be required to be parties if the agreement were then being made, and any reference in this Act to the parties to a sharing agreement shall be construed, as respects anything done at a subsequent time, as referring to the said persons.

(10) A sharing agreement may be amended by agreement of the parties thereto and with the consents that would then be required to a new sharing agreement.

2. – (1) Where a sharing agreement is made with respect to an existing or proposed church building which is to be owned or continue to be owned by one only of the sharing Churches, the trusts or purposes on or for which the building is held or to be held shall include the purposes and provisions of the agreement, as for the time being in force, and any instrument declaring those trusts and purposes shall be deemed to have effect, or (in the case of a proposed building) shall provide, accordingly. Trusts of shared church buildings.

(2) Where a sharing agreement is made with respect to an existing or proposed church building which is to be owned jointly by all or some of the sharing Churches, that ownership shall be effected by vesting the building in trustees representing those Churches, or in a custodian trustee with managing trustees representing those Churches, to be held on trust to be used for the purposes of the sharing agreement and in accordance with its terms and, subject thereto, for such other charitable purposes of the sharing Churches as may be appropriate, and the trust instrument relating to the building shall provide accordingly.

(3) The body or person in whom an exsiting church building is vested shall have power, notwithstanding any statutory or other legal provision, to convey the building to the managing trustees or custodian trustee aforesaid, for such consideration (if any) as may be provided in the sharing agreement or determined thereunder.

(4) The references in this section to a custodian trustee shall, subject to the making of such an order as is required by the Charities Act 1960 for the vesting of property in the official custodian for charities, including references to the said custodian. 1960 c. 58.

(5) The purposes of a sharing agreement shall be limited to purposes which are exclusively charitable according to the law of England and Wales.

3. – (1) A sharing agreement shall make provision with respect to the financial and other obligations of the parties thereto in respect of the provision, improvement and management of the church building or buildings shared or to be shared under the agreement, and the powers of any body or person under any statutory or other legal provision to apply money, whether by grant or loan, in respect of the provision, improvement or management of church buildings of a Church Financial and management provisions.

to which this Act applies shall be applicable in like manner in respect of any church building shared or to be shared by that Church under a sharing agreement.

(2) The powers of any body or person under any statutory or other legal provision –

(a)   to acquire, hold, improve or manage church buildings of a Church to which this Act applies, or any property to be used for or in connection with the provision of such church buildings, or

(b)   to grant property for or in connection with the provision of such church buildings, whether for a full consideration or for less than a full consideration,

shall be applicable in like manner in respect of any church building to which a sharing agreement relates and which, under the agreement, is or is to be owned by that Church or jointly owned by that Church and any other Church or Churches, and any such power to hold church buildings shall include a power to be a trustee (representing that Church) of such a jointly owned church building or, in the case of a corporation aggregate, to be the custodian trustee thereof.

1954 No. 1.

1943 No. 1

(3) The powers of the Church Commissioners under the New Housing Areas (Church Buildings) Measure 1954, and the powers of the said Commissioners and certain other bodies and persons under section 13 and 14 of the New Parishes Measure 1943 (which relate to the provision and improvement of church buildings), shall not be applicable for the purposes mentioned in the foregoing provisions of this section except as may be provided by a Measure of the [¹General Synod] extending the said Measures.

(4) The responsibility for the management of a church building owned by one only of the sharing Churches under a sharing agreement and of its contents shall remain with the authorities of or trustees representing that Church, but that responsibility shall be discharged in accordance with the provisions of the agreement and any arrangements made thereunder, including provisions or arrangements for consultation with any other sharing Church and for the payment of contributions by any other sharing Church towards the expenses of management.

(5) Where a sharing agreement provides for the joint ownership of the shared building by all or some of the sharing

¹Words substituted by virtue of Synodical Government Measure 1969 (No. 2), s. 2(1).

Churches, the responsibility of the trustees for the management of the building shall be in place of any responsibility of the authorities of the sharing Churches as respects that building, including responsibility under any statutory or other legal provision:

Provided that –

(a) the trustees shall discharge that responsibility in accordance with the provisions of the sharing agreement and any arrangements made thereunder, including provisions or arrangements for consultation with any sharing Church which is not a joint owner and for the payment of contributions by the sharing Churches towards the expenses of management;

(b) the agreement may provide that any moveables required for the worship of any sharing Church shall be the responsibility of the authorities of that Church.

(6) In this section "management", in relation to a church building, includes the repair and furnishing of the building.

4. – (1) A sharing agreement shall make provision, in the case of a building used as a place of worship, for determining the extent to which it is to be available for worship in accordance with the forms of service and practice of the sharing Churches respectively, and may provide for the holding of such joint services on such occasions as may be approved by those Churches, and may dispense, to such extent as may be necessary, with the requirement to hold certain services of the Church of England on Sundays and other days.

Sharing of church buildings for purposes of worship.

(2) Notwithstanding any statutory or other legal provision, a minister, reader or lay preacher of one of the Churches sharing a church building under a sharing agreement may, by invitation of a minister, reader or lay preacher of another such Church, take part in conducting worship in that building in accordance with the forms of service and practice of that other Church; but the rights given by this subsection shall be exercised in accordance with any rules or directions given by either Church and to any limitation imposed by or under the sharing agreement.

(3) Subject to the foregoing provisions of this section, the participation of the communities of the sharing Churches in each other's worship shall be governed by the practices and disciplines of those Churches in like manner as if they worshipped in separate buildings.

5. – (1) A sharing agreement shall not be made with respect to an existing consecrated church of the Church of England unless –

(a) the church will under the agreement remain in the sole ownership of the Church of England; or

(b) authority to make the agreement on behalf of the Church of England is given by a pastoral scheme under the Pastoral Measure 1968 as extended for the purpose by a subsequent Measure of the [¹General Synod], and the church will under the agreement be in the joint ownership of the Church of England and another Church or Churches.

(2) Where a sharing agreement is made on behalf of the Church of England with respect to a church building used or to be used as a place of worship, but not an existing consecrated church, the building shall not be consecrated unless it will under the agreement be in the sole ownership of the Church of England.

(3) Where a sharing agreement relates to a consecrated church, the faculty jurisdiction shall not apply in respect of moveables required for the worship of any sharing Church other than the Church of England.

(4) Where a church building being a place of worship is shared by the Church of England under a sharing agreement:–

(a) if the agreement provides for the sole ownership of the building by the Church of England, but not otherwise, the building may become or remain a parish church;

(b) in any case the agreement shall not prevent or affect the designation of the building as a parish centre of worship under section 29 of the Pastoral Measure 1968.

Solemnization of
marriages in shared or
other inter-
denominational
buildings.
1855 c. 81.
1949 c. 76.

6. – (1) A church building to which a sharing agreement relates (including a building in the sole ownership of the Church of England) may be certified under the Places of Worship Registration Act 1855 as a place of religious worship of any Church sharing the building other than the Church of England, and the provisions of the Marriage Act 1949 relating to the registration of buildings shall apply for and in relation to the registration of any such church building certified as aforesaid, subject to the modifications specified in Schedule 1 to this Act.

¹Words substituted by virtue of Synodical Government Measure 1969 (No. 2), s. 2(1).

(2) The provisions of the Marriage Act 1949 relating to the publication of banns and the solemnization of marriages according to the rites of the Church of England shall apply to a church building shared by the Church of England under a sharing agreement, and shall so apply notwithstanding that the building is registered under Part III of the Act, and accordingly –

(a) if the building is a parish church or parish centre of worship, the said provisions shall apply as they apply to other parish churches and parish centres of worship; and

(b) in any other case, section 20 of the said Act (which provides for the licensing of chapels for such publication and solemnization) shall apply.

(3) The proviso to section 26(2) of the said Act shall not apply to a church building to which a sharing agreement relates, except in respect of marriages to be solemnized according to the rites of the Church of England.

(4) Where a chapel of any university, college, school, hospital or other public or charitable institution, or a building held on trust for purposes of public worship but not a church building to which a sharing agreement relates, is used for the purposes of public worship in accordance with the forms of service and practice of two or more Churches to which this Act applies, the foregoing provisions of this section shall apply thereto in like manner as they apply to church buildings to which a sharing agreement relates, except that –

(a) the provisions of Schedule 1 other than paragraph 1 thereof shall not apply;

(b) in subsection (2)(b) of this section the reference to section 20 of the Marriage Act 1949 shall include a reference to section 21 of that Act.

(5) This section (except where it refers to parish centres of worship) shall apply to the Church in Wales in like manner as it applies to the Church of England.

7. – (1) Where a sharing agreement is made with respect to a church building or buildings proposed to be used under the agreement as a residence or residences for ministers or lay workers, the purpose of the agreement shall be to provide residential accommodation, whether in the form of separate residences or otherwise, available for occupation by the ministers or lay workers of the sharing Churches in accordance with arrangements made under the agreement.

Sharing of residential buildings.

(2) Where under any such agreement a separate residence is let to an incumbent of the Church of England in his corporate capacity, it shall be the residence house of the benefice during the term of the lease.

(3) A sharing agreement shall not be made with respect to an existing residence house of a benefice of the Church of England, unless authority to make the agreement on behalf of that Church is given by a pastoral scheme under the Pastoral Measure 1968 as extended for the purpose by a subsequent Measure of the [¹General Synod].

1968 No. 1

(4) No right of pre-emption, or provision for the property to revert to previous ownership, shall be exercisable or operate on the conveyance, vesting or disposal of such an existing residence house under section 2 or section 9 of this Act (except section 9(4)).

Application to shared buildings of certain provisions of Charities Act 1960.
1960 c. 58.

8. – (1) A sharing agreement with respect to any church building shall not affect any exception or exemption for the building from any provisions of the Charities Act 1960.

(2) A sharing agreement with respect to any church building which under the agreement is owned by the Church of England shall not affect the application to the building of section 45(2) of the Charities Act 1960 (which excludes from the definition of "charity" certain corporations of the Church of England in respect of their corporate property and certain trusts of consecrated property).

(3) Section 29 of the Charities Act 1960 (which requires dealings with charity property to be authorised by an order of the court or the Charity Commissioners) shall not apply to the conveyance, vesting or disposal of church buildings under section 2 or section 9 of this Act.

Termination of sharing.

9. – (1) A sharing agreement shall contain provisions for terminating the sharing of the church building or buildings, and such provisions may –

(a) if the agreement relates to two or more buildings, provide for terminating the sharing of any building before the others; and

(b) if there are two or more sharing Churches, provide for the withdrawal of any Church from the sharing of any church building, not being a Church which is the sole owner or previous owner of the building;

---

¹Words substituted by virtue of Synodical Government Measure 1969 (No. 2), s. 2(1).

and the sharing agreement may make provision for financial adjustments as between the Churches, on such termination or withdrawal, by payments out of moneys held for the purposes of the sharing agreement or of any shared building or by other payments by one Church to another.

(2) On the termination of the sharing of a church building owned by one only of the sharing Churches, the building shall be held on the trusts or for the purposes on or for which it was held before the sharing agreement or would be held but for the sharing agreement.

(3) On the termination of the sharing of a church building jointly owned by all or some of the sharing Churches, being a building which before the sharing agreement was owned by one only of the Churches, the building shall, without any conveyance or other assurance, vest as follows:–

(a) if the building was previously a consecrated church of the Church of England or a building (other than a consecrated church) vested in the incumbent of a Church of England parish, it shall vest in the incumbent of the parish in which the building is then situated, for the same purposes as before, as nearly as may be;

(b) in any other case, it shall vest in such of the trustees in whom the building is vested as represent the Church who previously owned the building or, if the building is vested in a custodian trustee, it shall remain so vested but be managed by such of the managing trustees as represent that Church, and it shall be held and managed on the trusts or for the same purposes as before, as nearly as may be.

(4) Where the sharing of a church building jointly owned as aforesaid but not previously owned by one only of the sharing Churches is terminated, the sharing agreement and the trust instrument may provide for the disposal of the building (including disposal to one of the sharing Churches) and for the application of the proceeds to charitable purposes of the sharing Churches.

10. – (1) No sharing agreement shall be made with respect to a cathedral church or peculiar of the Church of England or any church building of that Church situated in an extra-diocesan or extra-parochial place. ^{Cathedrals, peculiars, extra-diocesan and extra-parochial churches of the Church of England.}

(2) The dean or provost and chapter of such a cathedral church may, notwithstanding any statutory or other legal provision, authorise a chapel or other part of the cathedral

67

church to be used for the purposes of public worship in accordance with the forms of service and practice of two or more Churches to which this Act applies, and section 6 of this Act shall apply to any such chapel or part of a cathedral church in like manner as it applies to a chapel of any such institution as is mentioned in subsection (4) of that section.

(3) Nothing in this section shall be taken as preventing a church building in an extra-diocesan or extra-parochial place being used, otherwise than in pursuance of a sharing agreement, by two or more Churches to which this Act applies, or as preventing the application of section 6(4) of this Act to such a church building.

Churches to which this Act applies, and appropirate authorities thereof.

11. – (1) The Churches to which this Act applies are the Churches specified in the first column of Schedule 2 to this Act, the Church of England and all other Churches who give notice under subsection (3) of this section.

(2) The expression "appropriate authority", in relation to each of the Churches specified in the first column of Schedule 2 to this Act, means the authority specified in the second column of the Schedule in respect of that Church, and if different authorities are specified in relation to different provisions of this Act, means in each provision the authority specified in relation thereto.

(3) Any Church for the time being represented on the General Council of the British Council of Churches or on the governing body of the Evangelical Alliance or the British Evangelical Council may give notice in writing to the General Secretary of the British Council of Churches or as the case may be of the governing body concerned, that it desires that this Act should apply to that Church, and the notice shall specify the appropriate authority or authorities of that Church for the purposes of this Act, and the General Secretary concerned shall publish in the *London Gazette* a notice signed by him –

(*a*) stating that the Church concerned is represented on the said General Council or governing body and has expressed its desire that this Act should apply to that Church;

(*b*) stating that this Act will apply to that Church as from the date of publication of the notice; and

(*c*) specifying the appropriate authority or authorities of that Church for the purposes of this Act;

and thereupon this Act shall apply to that Church as from that date and shall have effect as if an entry in respect of that

Church and the appropriate authority or authorities so specified were made in Schedule 2 thereto.

12. – (1) In this Act, unless the context otherwise requires, Interpretation.

"building" includes a part of a building;

"church building" means a building used or proposed to be used by a Church or Churches to which this Act applies–

(a) as a place of worship;

(b) as a church hall or centre available wholly or mainly for activities other than worship;

(c) as a youth club or centre or youth hostel;

(d) as a residence or residences for ministers or lay workers;

Provided that –

(i) a sharing agreement may provide for including any land (other than land used or appropriated for use for burials) or outbuildings held or to be held with a church building, and any easements or rights enjoyed or to be enjoyed with a church building, and references to a church building shall in relation to that agreement, be construed accordingly;

(ii) the said expression shall not include any school;

"consecrated" means consecrated for the purpose of public worship according to the rites and ceremonies of the Church of England;

"Diocesan Board of Finance" means the Board of that name constituted under the Diocesan Board of Finance Measure 1925 for that diocese: 1925 No. 3

Provided that, if the bishop certifies that a board of finance not so constituted or a body constituted for the holding on trust of diocesan property is to be treated for the purposes of this Measure as the Diocesan Board of Finance for that diocese, the board or body so certified shall be so treated:

"Diocesan Education Committee" means a committee constituted in accordance with the Schedule to the Diocesan Education Committees Measure 1955 or in accordance with an order made by the Secretary of State under that Measure; 1955 No. 1 (4 & 5 Eliz. 2).

"statutory or other legal provision" means any Act or Measure, any instrument or document made or having effect under or by virtue of any Act or Measure, any other instrument or document affecting legal rights or obligations, any trust

(whether arising under a trust instrument or otherwise), and any rule of law, being an Act, Measure, instrument, document, trust, or rule in force at the passing of this Act:
Provided that the said expression shall not include a lease or tenancy of a church building or any mortgage, charge, covenant or rights affecting a church building and operating for the benefit of persons other than a Church to which this Act applies, or any general Act of Parliament regulating or affecting the use of land.

(2) For the purposes of this Act, a church building shall be deemed to be owned by a Church if the building is held by any body or person, whether for a freehold or leasehold estate, for purposes of that Church or on behalf of that Church, and, in the case of a leasehold building, any reference to the conveyance or vesting of the building shall be construed as a reference to the conveyance or vesting of the leasehold estate.

(3) If it is certified by the Church Commissioners that the ownership of a consecrated church of the Church of England cannot be ascertained with certainty, and that the church ought to be treated as vested in the incumbent of the parish in which it is situated, the church shall be deemed for the purposes of this Act to be so vested.

(4) Any reference in this Act to any Act or Measure shall be construed as a reference to that Act or Measure as amended by any subsequent Act or Measure.

Saving for temporary loans of church buildings.

13. Nothing in this Act shall be taken as affecting any practice of a Church to which this Act applies of lending church buildings temporarily for particular occasions to other religious bodies.

Extent.

14. – (1) This Act shall extend to church buildings in England and Wales.

(2) This Act may be extended to church buildings in the Isle of Man by an Act of Tynwald, and shall then have effect, in relation to such buildings, subject to such exemptions, adaptations or modifications as may be specified in that or a subsequent Act of Tynwald.

Short title.

15. This Act may be cited as the Sharing of Church Buildings Act 1969.

SCHEDULES

SCHEDULE 1 Section 6.

MODIFICATIONS OF PROVISIONS OF THE MARRIAGE ACT 1949
RELATING TO THE REGISTRATION OF BUILDINGS, IN THEIR
APPLICATION TO SHARED CHURCH BUILDINGS

1. A church building to which a sharing agreement relates may be registered under section 41 of the Marriage Act 1949 (hereinafter referred to as "the Act") notwithstanding that it is not a separate building or deemed to be a separate building within the meaning of that section. 1949 c. 76.

2. An application under the said section 41 shall be made by a representative (as hereinafter defined) of a sharing Church other than the Church of England, and, if there are two or more such Churches, the registration shall be deemed to have been made on behalf of the congregations of all those Churches, whether or not their representatives joined in the application.

3. Where a sharing Church other than the Church of England withdraws from the sharing of a registered church building, which continues to be used by another such Church, the registration shall not be cancelled.

4. An authorisation and certification of a person under section 43(1) of the Act to be present at the solemnization of marriages in a church building to which a sharing agreement relates shall be effected by a representative of a sharing Church other than the Church of England, and, if there are two or more such sharing Churches, different persons may be so authorised and certified on behalf of those Churches, but each such person shall be an authorised person for the purposes of the Act in respect of the solemnization of any marriage in that building; and references in the Act to authorised persons and their certification shall be construed accordingly.

5. The proviso added to the said section 43(1) by the Marriage Acts Amendment Act 1958, which prescribes a period of twelve months before a person may be authorised as aforesaid, shall not apply to any authorisation under this Schedule, and, if a sharing Church withdraws, in the circumstances mentioned in paragraph 3 above, from the sharing of a registered church building, the registration shall, for the purpose of the application of the said proviso to another building registered on behalf of the congregation of the withdrawing Church, be deemed to have been cancelled at the time of the withdrawal. 1958 c. 29

6. The consent required under the proviso to section 44(1) of the Act shall, if the marriage is to be solemnized according to the rites of a sharing Church, be given by the minister ordinarily responsible for the conduct of worship by the congregation of that Church or, if the sharing Church is not the Roman Catholic Church, by a representative of that sharing Church, and in the case of other marriages shall be given by one of the trustees, owners or managers of the building.

7. The appointment of two or more authorised persons in respect of the same building shall not require any additional set or sets of duplicate marriage register books to be supplied for that building, and regulations made under section 74 of the Act may make provision with respect to the custody and use of the register books and the returns to be made by the authorised persons of the entries therein, and may make any necessary modifications of the provisions of the Act relating to those matters.

8. Nothing in this Schedule shall affect any registration or authorisation which is in force when a sharing agreement takes effect in respect of the building concerned, and any such registration or authorisation shall continue in force and have effect as if it had been made under this Schedule.

9. In this Schedule "representative", in relation to a Church Sharing a church building, means –

(a) if the building is jointly owned, a trustee representing that Church;

(b) in any other case, a party to the agreement on behalf of that Church.

Section 11.

SCHEDULE 2

CHURCHES AND THEIR APPROPRIATE AUTHORITIES

Name of Church	Appropriate Authority or Authorities
Any Church of the Baptist Denomination	As respects section 1(3) and (4), the Baptist Trust Corporation as hereinafter defined, acting with the concurrence of the Church meeting. As respects section 1(8), the Baptist Trust Corporation.
Any Church of the Congregational Denomination.	As respects section 1(3) and (4), the Congregational Trust Corporation as hereinafter defined, acting with the concurrence of the Church meeting.

72

As respects section 1(8), the Congregational Trust Corporation.

Any Congregation of the Association of Churches of Christ in Great Britain and Ireland.	As respects section 1(3) and (4), the Annual Conference of the Association of Churches of Christ acting with the concurrence of the duly constituted Church meeting. As respects section 1(8), the Annual Conference of the Association of Churches of Christ.
The Methodist Church	The Annual Conference of the Methodist Church.
['The United Reformed Church	The Synod of the province of the United Reformed Church in which the church or buildings is or are or will be situated.]
The Roman Catholic Church	The Bishop of the diocese in which the church building or buildings is or are or will be situated.
The Church in Wales	The Governing Body of the Church in Wales.

For the purposes of this Schedule, "the Baptist Trust Corporation" and "the Congregational Trust Corporation" have the following meanings:

(a) if the church building or buildings to which the sharing agreement concerned relates is or are or will be vested in a Baptist or Congregational Trust Corporation within the meaning of the Baptist and Congregational Trusts Act 1951, it means that Corporation;   1951 c. xvii.

(b) otherwise it means the Baptist or Congregational Trust Corporation (within the meaning of the said Act) in whose area of operations the church building or buildings is or are or will be situated, or if there is more than one such Corporation, the one determined by the Church meeting.

---

1 Words substituted by United Reformed Church Act 1972 (c. xviii)

Appendix IV
Bibliography
(in chronological order of publication)

Gillian Carver: **A Place to Meet:** The use of church property and the New Religious Minorities in Britain, BCC 1978.

Coming Together in Christ/Building Together in Christ: The first and second reports of the joint working party between white-led and black-led churches, BCC, 1978.

The Holy Communion, Commission of Covenanted Churches in Wales, 1981 (ecumenical rite).

Local Churches in Covenant, Roman Catholic Committee for Christian Unity, 1984.

With Charity and With Conviction – Baptists in local partnership with other Christians in England, 1984.

Ministry in Local Ecumenical Projects, BCC 1985.

Local Church Unity: Guidelines for Local Ecumenical Projects and Sponsoring Bodies, BCC 1985.

A Question of Use: Sharing the Premises and Sharing the Gospel, Methodist Church Property Division.

Tony Holden, **People, Churches and Multi-Racial Projects,** Methodist Church Division of Social Responsibility, 1985.

Stewards of God's House: Christian Stewardship and Church Buildings, BCC 1988.

Hugh Cross, **Guidebook for Members of Sponsoring Bodies and Ecumenical Councils,** BCC 1988.

Ecumenical Relations: Canons B43 and B44 Code of Practice. General Synod of the Church of England, 1989.

Church in Wales Ecumenical Canons, 1990.

Basil Hazledine, A Harmony of Church Administration, BCC 1990.

Patterns of Sharing and Commitment between Methodist and United Reformed Churches, sixth edition, 1990.

David Douglas, The Handbook of the International Ministerial Council of Great Britain, IMCGB 1990.

Baptism, Commission of Covenanted Churches in Wales, 1990, (ecumenical rite).

Canllawiau ar gyfer Gweinidogaeth Bro, Guidelines for Neighbourhood Ministries, Interdenominational Consultative Committee on Ministry, Wales 1992.

Register of Local Ecumenical Projects in Wales, CYTUN/ENFYS, 1991 (in process of revision).

Confirmation and Re-Affirmation of Baptismal Faith, Joint Liturgical Group, 1992 (ecumenical rite).

Register of Local Ecumenical Projects and Sponsoring Bodies, Churches Together in England, 1993.

Constitutional Guidelines for a Local Ecumenical Project, Revised 1993, Churches Together in England.

Guidelines for the Review of Local Ecumenical Projects, Revised 1993, Churches Together in England.

This includes both earlier documents consulted by the Working Group and material currently in print for further reference.

Appendix V

Members of the Working Group which prepared these Revised Guidelines:

Mrs. Jenny Carpenter

Churches Together in England,
Field Officer (North and Midlands)
and Secretary, Churches Together
in England's Group for Local Unity

The Revd. Dr. Colin Davey

Council of Churches for Britain
and Ireland, Co-ordinating
Secretary for Church Life

The Rt. Revd. Paul Hackman

First Pentecostal Regional Bishop
of International Ministerial
Council of Great Britain and
Bishop of Beneficial Christ Church

The Very Revd. Archimandrite
Maximos Lavriotis

Archdiocese of Thyateira and
Great Britain (Greek Orthodox)

The Revd. Rodney Matthews

CYTUN: Churches Together in
Wales, Secretary, Commission on
Ecumenical Affairs

Mr. Derek Taylor Thompson

Secretary, Churches' Main
Committee

The Rt. Revd. Howard Tripp

Roman Catholic Auxiliary Bishop
of Southwark and Moderator of
Churches Together in England's
Group for Local Unity

The Working Group consulted widely with legal and property advisers to the Churches and with denominational and county ecumenical officers in the course of revising these Guidelines.